THE
EXTRAORDINARY
CEO

THE
EXTRAORDINARY
CEO

DOUGLAS C. EADIE

asae

American Society of Association Executives

WASHINGTON, D.C.

Information in this book is accurate as of the time of publication and consistent with standards of good practice in the general management community. As research and practice advance, however, standards may change. For this reason, it is recommended that readers evaluate the applicability of any recommendation in light of particular situations and changing standards.

American Society of Association Executives
1575 I Street, NW
Washington, D.C. 20005
Phone: (202) 626-2723
Fax: (202) 408-9634
E-mail: books@asaenet.org

George Moffat, Publisher
Linda Munday, Director of Book Publishing
Anna Nunan, Book Acquisitions Coordinator
Zachary Dorsey, Production Coordinator
Cover and interior design by Troy Scott Parker, Cimarron Design

Library of Congress Cataloging-in-Publication Data

Eadie, Douglas C.
    The extraordinary CEO / Douglas C. Eadie.
    p.   cm.
    ISBN 0-88034-156-4
    1. Chief executive officers. 2. Directors of corporations.
 3. Executive ability. 4. Leadership. 5. Boards of directors.
 6. Corporate governance. I. Title.
 HD38.2.E17   1999
 658.4'092—dc21   99-28132
                                        CIP

Printed in the United States of America.

10 9 8 7 6 5 4 3 2 1

This book is available at a special discount when ordered in bulk quantities. For information, contact the ASAE Member Service Center at (202) 371-0940.

A complete catalog of titles is available on the ASAE home page at http://www.asaenet.org.

To

Professor and Mrs. Nathan D. Grundstein

with Deep Appreciation for Your Friendship

and Unfailingly Wise Counsel

Contents

Acknowledgments

THE THEMES OF *The Extraordinary CEO* draw heavily on my quarter-century of work with nonprofit organizations of all shapes and sizes, including a diverse array of associations. But I am only the proximate cause—not the sole author—of this book. I must acknowledge the important contributions of the hundreds of nonprofit chief executive officers with whom I have worked over the years. They have taught me most of what I know about leading change, and they have truly earned the title "Extraordinary CEO."

My teachers have also included the thousands of nonprofit board members who have participated in my planning workshops and retreats and the senior managers who have loyally, and without fanfare, labored to translate good intentions into concrete change in their associations.

From 1996 to 1998, I was privileged to serve on the Executive Management Section Council of the American Society of Association Executives (ASAE). My participation in the council's exploration of the education and training needs of association executives strengthened my understanding of the CEO "business" and enriched the ideas in this book. My colleagues on the council, and the ASAE vice president who serves as its chief staff, Paul Meyer, also deserve credit for much of what is good and useful about *The Extraordinary CEO*.

Certain association CEOs have strongly influenced my thinking on matters related to change leadership and management, and I owe them special thanks. They are Robert Betz, executive director of the Health Industry Group Purchasing Association, Washington, D.C.; Thomas Bowman, CAE, president & CEO of the Association for Investment Management & Research, Charlottesville, Va.; Ken

Crerar, president of the Council of Insurance Agents & Brokers, Washington, D.C.; S. Wayne Kay, president & CEO of the Health Industry Distributors Association, Alexandria, Va.; Linda Kloss, executive director & CEO of the American Health Information Management Association, Chicago; and Gregory Maciag, president & CEO of the Agency-Company Organization for Research and Development, Pearl River, N.Y. *The Extraordinary CEO* contains practical examples from the large-scale change programs these CEOs have led.

Several association CEOs and senior executives gave generously of their time to advise me on the major themes of this book. I am indebted to: Carol Aten, senior vice president of the National Parks and Conservation Association, Washington, D.C.; David Brugger, president & CEO of the Association of America's Public Television Stations, Washington, D.C.; Anne Bryant, executive director of the National School Board Association, Alexandria, Va.; Stephen Crane, executive vice president of the American Academy of Physician Assistants, Alexandria, Va.; William Dodge, executive director of the National Association of Regional Councils, Washington, D.C.; Cynthia Fisher, former director of education of the International Association of Convention and Visitor Bureaus, Washington, D.C.; David Feild, former executive vice president & CEO of the American College of Cardiology; Jeffrey Finkle, president of the National Council for Urban Economic Development, Washington, D.C.; Paul Greeley, CAE, president of the American Chamber of Commerce Executives, Alexandria, Va.; Dr. Paul Houston, executive director of the American Association of School Administrators, Arlington, Va.; Gail Kincaide, CAE, executive director of the Association of Women's Health, Obstetric & Neonatal Nurses, Washington, D.C.; William Millar, president of the American Public Transit Association, Washington, D.C.; Dr. Margaret Miller, president of the American Association for Higher Education, Washington, D.C.; James Morley, president of the National Association of College and University Business Officers, Washington, D.C.; and Dr. David Pierce, president of the American Association of Community Colleges, Washington D.C.

More than 30 years ago, Professor Nathan D. Grundstein founded and for several years directed an extraordinary educational program at Case Western Reserve University in Cleveland. I was fortunate to spend a year as one of Professor Grundstein's fellows in the graduate program in Public Management Science (PMS). Always insightful and challenging, never predictable, and often quite entertaining, the feisty

Professor Grundstein opened for the fellows in the PMS program intellectual paths they might travel in the quest of a more fundamental intelligence of the world and a clearer vision of the infinite possibilities open to the intrepid traveler.

Professor Grundstein has, in the years since I was his student, continued to serve as a mentor, wise counselor, and vocal enemy of any tendency of mine to rest in the comfortable embrace of yesterday's knowing. Most important of all, I have had the pleasure of his and his wife Dorothy's friendship all these years. The words in this book are not his, but he is one of the important co-authors nonetheless.

Linda Munday, director of book publishing, and Anna Nunan, acquisitions editor, at ASAE, have for this book, as for others we have worked on together over the years, provided insightful and practical advice and counsel relative to both style and content. There is no question that this is a far better book because they had a hand in its creation. Candy Korn's very capable editorial assistance also contributed to the quality of the final manuscript.

My children, Jennifer and William, are a constant source of wonder, joy, and inspiration as they explore their own creative frontiers and lead change in their own lives. And finally, I owe a tremendous debt to my wife, confidante, and steadfast supporter, Barbara Krai. Her unconditional love and unfailing encouragement and support helped me to find the energy to write this book in the midst of running a demanding business. Her critical reading of the text—wearing the hat of innovative business owner and entrepreneur—has made this a much more practitioner-friendly book than it might otherwise have been.

I alone, of course, am accountable for any shortcomings the reader may find in *The Extraordinary CEO*.

> – Douglas C. Eadie
> *Cleveland, Ohio*
> *April 1999*

Introduction

YOU'RE READY TO MOVE UP!

If you are reading this book, you are most likely a chief executive officer (CEO) or a CEO-aspirant now toiling away in the executive ranks. At the outset, let's agree that the CEO is the highest-ranking staff member of the association, is appointed by—and reports to—the board, and is responsible for all internal operations of the association.

Almost always a full-time employee, the CEO is typically called the "president and CEO" or the "executive director." Less often, and somewhat misleadingly, an association CEO is called "executive vice president." Whatever his or her working title, the association CEO is never the volunteer chair of the association board.

As a CEO or CEO-aspirant, you are undoubtedly highly accomplished in your work; otherwise, you would not be sitting in the seat you are in now. You have surely mastered the details of the particular business that your trade or professional association is in. You most likely know technical management functions and skills inside-out—operational planning and budget development, financial planning and management, human resource development, performance management, membership recruitment and retention, and the like.

To have reached this point in your career, you are quite disciplined and a skillful manager of time. You excel at making sure that your association satisfies its members and other customers, that its products and services are high quality, and that its operations are on time and within budget. You can probably write the Queen's English and acquit yourself well on the podium. And you have very likely developed strong leadership skills, too. You are good at articulating your vision of the desired future and know how to get the team excited about tackling new challenges.

In short, if you are reading this book, you are probably an ambitious, high-achieving, successful CEO or CEO-aspirant who is worth every penny you are paid. But you cannot assume that your future—and your association's future—is secure, no matter how well everything appears to be going. The price of complacency can be expensive—perhaps your association's precipitous decline, if not its extinction. So, you owe it to yourself and to your association to move to the next leadership plateau—to become an extraordinary CEO. Doing so will help ensure that your association will not only survive, but also thrive and grow, in the twenty-first century.

The Extraordinary CEO provides you with practical, down-to-earth guidance in helping your association develop two capacities that are critical to its success in today's changing, challenging times. One is *the capacity to govern,* primarily through a board whose members are fully engaged in providing strong strategic and policy leadership and through a close, positive working partnership between the board and CEO. The second is the *capacity to lead and manage association change* systematically by employing a new tool called "change portfolio management."

The Extraordinary CEO also tells you how to build two essential, individual capacities: *the capacity to empower and inspire your people* and *the capacity to bring your total intelligence to bear on leading your association.* You will come to rely not only on your intellect and reasoning capacity but also on a deeper self-knowledge.

Sweeping Transformations

In a stable world experiencing slow and predictable change, you might be able to rest on your laurels a bit, trusting that the leadership you have provided in building a smoothly operating, fiscally sound association will suffice as the twenty-first century arrives. Yet the odds are overwhelmingly against it. The world is anything but stable these days and for the foreseeable future. Even though change is nothing new in human affairs, seldom if ever in history has it been of such magnitude, so fast paced, or so unpredictable—and, hence, so challenging.

Of course, change can be beneficial to associations. Advances in electronic communication, for example, facilitate information exchange and decision making and save on postage and travel expenses. Potential members can learn about your association from your Web site—quickly, easily, inexpensively. Board committees with members scattered all over the country can meet and accomplish much via teleconferencing or videoconferencing. E-mail gets the word out instantaneously to members or state directors around the country.

However, unless they directly affect the content of your association's products and services or significantly lower your costs, technological advances basically speed up the management of *what is*. More often than not, talking on your cell phone or tap-tap-tapping on your laptop in your airline seat keeps you busier doing operational things faster and offers virtually no strategic advantage.

Change can be unsettling and threatening to associations. It may make organization structures obsolete and call into question such fundamentals as the size and shape of the industry or profession in which your members work, who your members are, and the core products and services you provide. Take, for example, the decline in volunteer time that has resulted from the dramatic growth in two-career families and the relatively busier schedules of the survivors of corporate downsizing. This development has left many associations with elaborate and often antiquated volunteer involvement structures that are too time intensive and cumbersome for today's harried volunteers.

For instance, one international association—the result of a merger of two associations—ended up with three boards: the "real" governing board and two shadow boards grandfathered from the two merging organizations, along with various councils, committees, and task forces. All harked back to a time when more volunteers had more time available. When such cumbersome structures remain in place, volunteer involvement tends to become ritualistic, dissatisfaction and frustration grow, and the CEO often gets blamed for all of the accumulated unhappiness.

More dramatic have been the sweeping transformations of entire industries, such as healthcare and financial services. Such fundamental reshaping of the business environment can call into question an association's mission, strategies, and membership. Increasingly, we see not only consolidation within an industry but also the emergence of new business organizations that blur the lines separating industries. For example, financial services firms now offer banking, insurance, and investment management. In healthcare, integrated managed care systems blur the distinctions between insurer and provider.

In such a topsy-turvy world, how does an association of health product distributors deal with the metamorphosing health markets? What about an association of property/casualty insurance agents and brokers: Does it re-design itself as an association of financial services firms? These questions are not the stuff of ho-hum operational management.

Masters of the Change Game

In this rambunctious, challenging, and often threatening world, doing a virtuoso job of leading and managing what already exists simply will not do. To rise to the next level of CEO leadership—to become an extraordinary CEO—you must diversify and enrich your portfolio of CEO leadership goals, skills, and attributes. The core technical competencies, while still important, focus on managing and controlling what is. The world of the future places a premium on innovating and leading change in response to the change going on around us.

Above all else, the extraordinary CEO is the master of the change game. The extraordinary CEO is in the business of preparing associations to meet the tremendous change challenges facing them. He or she is the association's preeminent change champion.

Associations that are most likely to survive and thrive in this challenging world are:

- Governed by a board that fully involves its members in providing strategic leadership and goes well beyond reviewing and reacting to staff recommendations.
- Capable of initiating and leading their own innovation and change efforts, not simply reacting to crises.
- Led by a CEO who empowers the people in the association, inspires their loyalty and trust, and brings his or her total intelligence to bear in leading.

Governance

Your board is the most precious resource you have as an association CEO, and your board is an indispensable partner in leading and managing change. Think about it. You have surely noticed that the typical board member is a bright, ambitious, high-achieving volunteer who brings to the board room not only the will to do good, but also substantial high-level experience, executive expertise, diverse perspectives, and far-flung networks.

Board members not only bring vital intelligence to the process of developing your association's strategic change portfolio, they also supply critical legitimacy and financial support during the process of implementing the "change chunks" that make up the portfolio.

Despite the tremendous promise of boards, in practice they tend not to work well, for various reasons; the most important of which is the failure to develop a detailed board governance design. If you want your board to be a powerful, positive partner in leading change, you must help your board develop its own design for leading. Volunteers seldom have the time to undertake the job alone, nor should they be expected to.

Leading and Managing Change

The concept of the strategic change portfolio is one of the most revolutionary developments in the history of nonprofit planning. You have probably learned that most planning that organizations do is intended to bring order and control to functions and programs. This is certainly true of operational planning and budget preparation, but it is true as well of traditional approaches to strategic planning, which often projects the present into the future—usually for some arbitrary period, such as three or five years—without producing much, if any, innovation and change. A more contemporary variation on the strategic planning theme, the strategic management process, is explicitly focused on developing and implementing the strategic change initiatives ("change chunks" in scientific parlance) that make up an association's strategic change portfolio.

What makes the strategic change portfolio such a powerful tool for you as a CEO is that it actually produces change (in the form of change chunks) to deal with issues that you, your board, and your managers have decided deserve serious attention *now*, above and beyond running the shop. These strategic change initiatives can deal with more externally focused issues relating to association members, products, services, revenues, or relationships, and they can deal with more internally focused issues relating to capacity building, such as strengthening board leadership or enhancing the planning process.

As you know, planned change (change chunks) does not implement itself, no matter how well crafted its implementation strategies are. In fact, significant, planned change is the rare exception that proves the rule. So, one of your most serious challenges as a CEO is to make sure that your association puts together a structure and process for managing its strategic change portfolio. This does not require fancy technology, but does demand considerable focus and discipline to prevent the inexorable pressures of day-to-day operations from overwhelming change.

Empowering and Inspiring Your People

In addition to discussing your role in building the two key association capacities that are a major focus of the extraordinary CEO, this book deals with critical aspects of your behavior that can have tremendous impact on your association's long-term success. This takes us well beyond technical skills and into the realms of leadership philosophy, psychological development, and what we call "character."

"Empowerment" is frequently used as a political rallying cry that has more to do with ideology than leadership and management. I use it in a more practical sense, to describe the process of ensuring that all the people in your association contribute to the fullest feasible extent to realizing your values, vision, and mission in practice. In other words, when you empower people, your association capitalizes on their intelligence, skills, expertise, creativity, and other resources. Empowerment is principally accomplished through the design and implementation of processes (such as planning) that enable people to participate in a meaningful fashion in producing important outcomes. You also empower people by developing their capacities, mainly through education, training, and on-the-job learning.

In today's world, there is little you can accomplish as an autocratic commander-in-chief of your association. The command-and-control approach is as useful today as the buggy whip was a decade after Ford's Model T became America's car. Today, if you aspire to be an extraordinary CEO, taking the initiative in building your association's capacity to lead change, you have no choice but to facilitate the participation of your board, volunteers, and senior managers in creating and managing the association's change portfolio. At the very least, this requires patience and self-discipline—as you resist the temptation to short-cut process with right answers, much less marching orders—

and perhaps at times even therapeutic skills, as you help people cope with the inevitable anxiety that people feel when they are involved in any kind of change.

You have an opportunity to inspire the people around you through rhetoric that calls to mind higher ends and purposes, but words usually have a limited impact unless they are backed by behavior that supports them. Your most powerful inspirational tool is your commitment to a set of core values that you teach by example and that you avoid contradicting in practice. This builds a strong emotional line of credit that helps pay for the tremendous demands of change.

Building Your Total Intelligence

Anyone reading this book is likely to be highly intelligent in the familiar sense: logical reasoning, rational decision making, setting goals, applying discipline in achieving them, and the like. These aspects of intelligence, which relate to the conscious mind, are certainly essential for successful CEO leadership. However, what goes on in the conscious mind when you think and reason does not make up a complete intelligence. Strong emotions that have to do with parts of your self residing in your subconscious mind can powerfully influence your behavior—often negatively. For example, you might react defensively to strong people around you who are not at all a real threat, thereby limiting their contribution to your association. Developing your total intelligence means gaining an understanding of those parts of your self that are hidden in your subconscious mind, making it less likely that negative emotions will control your behavior and limit your effectiveness as a CEO.

What Lies Ahead

This brief tour of the major themes of *The Extraordinary CEO* is intended to focus your mind and excite your interest in what lies ahead:

Chapter One provides you with detailed guidance in building your board's governing capacity and your working partnership with your board.

Chapter Two discusses how you can help your association build its capacity to lead and manage change.

Chapter Three describes practical ways that you can empower the people around you and inspire their trust and loyalty.

Chapter Four discusses how you can develop the total intelligence that strengthens your understanding of your self and limits the power of negative emotions to influence your leadership and apply that intelligence in your leadership work.

Chapter Five points you to sources of information on the subjects covered in this book.

THE
EXTRAORDINARY
CEO

Building the Capacity To Govern

As AN ASSOCIATION CEO, you'll never walk a finer line than when dealing with your governing board. On one hand, the board hired you and can fire you, and you are clearly expected to take direction from your board. On the other hand, boards are composed of part-time (and pressed-for-time) volunteers who typically have little familiarity with the field of governance. They're expected to provide overall direction to you and the association, but they're not always sure how best to accomplish that task. They're expected to develop their own capacity to govern but seldom have the time, knowledge, or inclination to do so.

Where do they look for answers? To you, the CEO.

It's only natural for you to take command of the board–CEO partnership. After all, you can't afford to let the board run amuck; nothing's more fearsome to contemplate than volunteers delving into matters that are best left to the professionals, right? But in taking command, you can easily assume total control—by keeping the board members busy reading and responding to finished staff work. A more creative and ultimately more productive approach is to help your board develop its own capacity to lead.

High Stakes, High Risk

Based on my work with hundreds of boards and their CEOs, I've concluded that the professional mortality rate of CEOs has more to do with their relationship with the board than with any other factor—in fact, there's no close second. Let's play out the control scenario (the "finished staff work" approach) and see why it's so high risk:

- Your board stays busy doing its nuts-and-bolts work of reviewing and commenting on staff work, during committee and board meetings. No one on the board has the time or inclination to consider how to improve what the board is doing or how to derive more satisfaction from it.
- You provide your board with the finished staff work board members seem to need and want, including well-crafted agendas and reports that are meticulously prepared.
- Your board, not deriving much satisfaction from merely reacting to staff initiatives, grows increasingly restive, frustrated, and maybe angry. Talk during meeting breaks begins to center around being a "staff driven" board. Board members don't become angry at themselves for failing to develop their capacity to govern. They hold you, the CEO, accountable for their dissatisfaction.

This is a common scenario, and if a CEO doesn't take action to break the downward spiral, the board–CEO partnership can erode beyond repair. Since in all of human history, so far as I can determine, no board has ever fired itself for poor governing performance, only one person will take the fall: the CEO. And in a way, if you've allowed yourself to get caught in this common trap, you deserve to suffer, because you've failed to play your part in the board–CEO partnership as fully and creatively as you can.

CEO Responsibility Redefined

What can you do to break the cycle? First and foremost, commit yourself to playing a more sophisticated role *vis-à-vis* your board. That means going well beyond guarding against board incursions into administrative territory. CEOs who have built the strongest, most positive working partnerships with their boards define their responsibility in this way:

I am responsible for helping my board develop its capacity to govern the association, make full use of the resources that board members bring, and ensure that the governing experience is satisfying and enjoyable. I can't do this job alone; the board must ultimately take accountability for its work. But I must help board members design their governing work, especially developing an effective process and structure. Indeed, I may even have to persuade them to undertake the design process.

I am accountable for helping my board become more accountable for its own work. It's a tremendous challenge, but I have no choice. Strong governance is critical to the association's long-term success, and a truly productive and satisfied board is critical to my professional longevity. In playing this role, I need to spend approximately one-quarter of my time on board affairs. I must remember that the board is, in a very real sense, my single most important "program," in addition to my taking responsibility for all association operations.

This is a new, demanding, and complex role for an association CEO to play. If you don't tackle it wholeheartedly and systematically, you may put your relationship with your board at risk and rob your association of the benefits that strong, proactive board leadership brings.

Governing in a Nutshell

Think of serving on a governing board as only one—albeit the most demanding and important—kind of volunteering in your association. Your association's members can also volunteer to serve in various technical advisory capacities—say, helping to put together the annual conference program or reviewing workshop proposals. They may often do some hands-on operational work, such as presenting testimony to a congressional committee or helping draft a new marketing plan.

It's important to keep the distinction between governing and other kinds of volunteering in mind. Association boards can fall into the trap of behaving like a technical advisory committee instead of actually governing. Many associations also make the mistake of using the "career ladder" approach to filling vacancies on their governing board: They assume that any volunteer work prepares association members to serve on the board. While nonboard volunteering may be evidence of commitment, it's not preparation for governing.

Governing is, by definition, the work of your association's governing board. Stripped down to the essentials, to govern means to make decisions of the highest importance for an association: decisions about where we are ultimately headed over the long run (our vision), what our basic purposes are (our mission), what values should guide our behavior, what rules should govern our activities (our policies), what innovation initiatives we should undertake, how much money we should spend on what programs this coming year, and the like. That's governing in a nutshell: making the most important decisions that determine what your association is all about and where it's going. Everything else—how often your board meets, what committees you employ, what board agendas look like, etc.—is a matter of designing how your board will go about making these preeminent governance decisions.

A Rich, Underused Resource

Board members bring impressive resources to the task of governing their associations. These resources include: the keen intelligence and analytical capacity that high-achieving people typically bring to their volunteer work; the wisdom and diverse perspectives that come from years of experience in governing and managing all kinds of for-profit and nonprofit enterprises; creativity and innovation skills; knowledge about approaches other organizations have taken in dealing with strategic and policy issues; and access to pertinent information on the external environment and to financial and other resources.

Board members also often bring specific professional and technical expertise, such as training in law or finance, that can enrich strategic and policy deliberations. Technical and professional expertise, however, is not a requirement for effective governing (although it is certainly pertinent to serving on a technical advisory committee).

In short, your board gives you access to a rich pool of resources that you can bring to bear on tackling the most important, high-stakes issues your association faces. Despite this tremendous potential, however, a great majority of nonprofit boards fall far short of their promise. To put it bluntly: *Most boards do not work.* Why? There are several reasons why boards are the most underexploited resource in American management:

- Only within the past fifteen years or so has the subject of governance been considered a top-level matter. Even today, if you go into a major bookstore, you'll be lucky to find more than three or four titles related to board governance. In contrast, you'll probably find that the books on executive leadership and management take up several shelves.

- The nonprofit world has been working with an outdated, negative model of board leadership, one that is largely passive–reactive and focused on damage control. Rather than seeing the board as a precious resource to be exploited in the interest of association vitality and growth, this traditional model basically sees the board as a body whose major role is to review and comment on finished staff work. Sitting at the pinnacle of the association structure, this kind of board receives and reacts to staff work, usually on paper, and provides the CEO with a yea or nay response.

This model also sees board members as capable of doing a lot of damage if they're not kept busy reading and reacting. There is the specter of the board's tentacles reaching out for responsibilities that rightly fall in the executive and administrative camp. This passive–reactive model undoubtedly contributes to the frustration, irritation, and anger that abound in board circles today.

Remember: Board members are usually high-achieving people who are accustomed to making a real difference in their lives outside the board. When they find themselves spending lots of time reading, being briefed, and merely responding, rather than leading, they naturally feel shortchanged.

Truly Working

Association boards that govern effectively have the following characteristics:

- They have embraced a new leadership model that goes well beyond the old review-and-comment approach. Instead, the board is seen as an organization that adds specific value to the association of which it is a part.

- They have fashioned a detailed design for governing, in keeping with this new leadership model. This design consists of three elements.

  – A leadership vision that broadly defines the board's leadership role.
  – A detailed definition of the products the board should devote significant time to producing (a governance mission).
  – A well-defined structure and process for producing these products.

- They take explicit accountability for managing their own performance and for developing themselves as a human resource.

- They work in close, active partnerships with their CEO, who provides strong support in carrying out their leadership design.

- Finally, keep in mind that aspiring CEOs are typically not educated or trained in working with boards. It's possible to earn a master's or doctoral degree in management without becoming well grounded in working with the boards you will encounter in real life. In addition, what is taught about boards is often the passive–reactive model that inevitably fails to work.

The New Model

Certainly, every board must continue to read, review, and comment on documents that staff prepare. But the new view of governing boards goes beyond this passive–reactive approach in seeing the board as an organization within the wider association. As a group of people working together to achieve a common purpose—in this case, governing—the board must contribute value to the association. So the key question you and your board need to ask is: What value—what outcomes and products—should our board spend significant time producing for the association?

If the answer is simply the traditional one—"Provide policy direction to the CEO and staff"—then we don't really have much of a handle on the board's work. There's nowhere you can take this kind of general response in terms of developing your board's leadership capacity. By contrast, the new view forces an association to explicitly design its board. This involves:

- Fashioning a broad leadership vision for the board that outlines the board's areas of influence and its role, and developing a detailed board governance mission. The latter identifies the key products the board intends to devote significant time to producing in major governance areas, such as planning and operational oversight.
- Fleshing out the structure and process required to produce these impacts and products.
- Ensuring that the board time, staff time, and other resources required to operate the board structure and process actually will be committed.

The idea of working with a board to design its governing role, in the context of the new view of board leadership, might appear radical and risky. You may find yourself conjuring up images of the damage a board can do when empowered to design itself. But my experience with hundreds of boards has proved just the opposite.

Boards that play an active role in their own design not only *don't* do damage, they become valuable partners of the CEO. Board members are happier and more satisfied, because they are engaged in doing well-defined work that is patently important; the value they add is clear. They are much more committed to their governing work because they really own it, having played an active role in creating their own leadership design. Fueling this process is volunteers' tremendous desire to contribute. I can count on one hand the number of board members over the past quarter-century who have been motivated to cause trouble. An overwhelming majority of volunteers who are tapped for board service really do want to make a positive contribution to their associations.

The board governance design process assumes that boards do not produce any impacts or products by themselves. Partnership—with the CEO, the management team, and other staff—is the name of the game. The design process doesn't aim at empowering a board to charge ahead on its own. Rather, it aims to pinpoint what the board should devote its time to producing—in partnership with the staff—and how it should go about producing it.

Getting Board Buy-In

Quick, inexpensive approaches to producing powerful results seldom work well, particularly when you're attempting a dramatic departure from past practice. Developing a board governance design is no exception. It's a rare board that would make significant changes in governance role, structure, and process just because you or a consultant recommended it or because you've put the board through a training program on being a better board.

The most effective approach to producing a design that will stand the test of time is to hold an intensive work session (or retreat) that lasts at least a full day, at which board members work through the different pieces of the design. Taking enough time to do the job right not only ensures that the design is technically workable and tailored to the unique needs and circumstances of your association, but also builds the kind of ownership on which implementation depends.

Only when people participate in-depth in creating something— whether a role, structure, or process—do they feel like owners of whatever has been created. Putting together an effective work session (or retreat) will be discussed later in this book; now let's look at how you can convince your board to participate at all in the design process.

If you go directly to your board and suggest setting aside a day or more for it to develop its own leadership design, you're likely to encounter lukewarm enthusiasm at best. One reason why board members won't have much of an appetite for the design process is that few, if any, of them will know what you're talking about. Many will think that such an exercise is an exotic luxury for which they don't have time. Since many boards have learned to suspect CEO motives, your pushing the idea of a work session yourself isn't likely to be the most effective approach.

Recognize that the idea of redesigning board governance is likely to be resisted by long-tenured board members who have labored mightily over the years to learn how to exert influence through the present board leadership process and structure. If only unconsciously, they are likely to feel threatened by the idea of redesigning how the board operates, fearing that all their pain and suffering have gone for naught. You can't realistically expect that they will feel enthusiastic about having to start all over again learning new ropes, and perhaps—God forbid!—failing and looking foolish.

Your newer board members are not likely to stand up and demand a voice in determining what the board produces and how it works, because the traditional process of assimilating new board members militates against this happening. New board members tend to dribble onto the board as individuals who are clearly expected to keep pretty quiet until they learn the ropes. Asking challenging questions, much less voicing any criticism of the way the board is operating, takes considerable courage. New board members typically are not provided with a detailed orientation on how the board works (rather, orientation tends to concentrate on the association's programs and finances) and are inundated with piles of paper that consume all of their time. Overwhelmed by the demands of learning the ropes, new board members don't have time to worry about whether they're the right ropes.

As the CEO, you need to fashion a sophisticated (and perhaps labyrinthine) strategy for overcoming resistance and persuading your board to design (or redesign) itself in a one- or two-day work session. Here are six strategies that may work well for you.

1. Make the choices clear. As you talk with your officers and other board members about the concept of a governance design, highlight the choices your board has.

The easiest and most natural choice is to inherit the role, structure, and process that have been in place on the board for several years. This choice fits the views that "A board is a board is a board" and "If it ain't broke, don't fix it." Emphasize that the inheritance approach means that what the board does and how it accomplishes its work have been determined by board members who are probably long gone.

The self-determination choice—to explicitly fashion a board governance design—ensures that the board's role, structure, and process reflect the priorities and expectations of current members of the board and the forces at work in the wider world. The operative principle is that what was developed in the past is highly unlikely to meet the needs of the present and the future.

2. Enlist the assistance of change champions. A change champion is someone who believes strongly in something and is willing to commit significant time and attention to achieving it. They are willing to go out on a limb publicly, thereby drawing other people along. Of course, the more influential the champions, the more likely they are to sway their colleagues' opinions.

An obvious starting point in recruiting change champions is the board's executive committee. Turning board officers into change champions for a board governance design process usually requires that they:

• Thoroughly understand the benefits of going through the process in terms that are meaningful to them. Rather than talking about improved governance in abstract terms, focus on how there will be much more to life on the board. Make clear that, through the design process, they can ensure that the board makes more important decisions and significantly influences association directions. As a result, being on the board will be more rewarding, satisfying, and fun. Keep in mind that individual benefits are always important, no matter what one says. I have found that people generally do care that their promotion of an initiative is likely to enhance their image as leaders among their colleagues.

- Have a firm grasp of the technical steps involved in the design process. They should understand what a governance vision is and how to produce it and know how to update board structure and process. No one wants to make a commitment to promote an approach that might not be technically feasible, risking the kind of mid-stream breakdown that would make them look foolish.
- See the design process as an opportunity to make a powerful contribution to board development. It must become the hallmark of their leadership, not just a CEO initiative. (For your part, you must be willing to have board leaders take the credit for coming up with the idea if you want them to truly own it.)

There are various approaches you can take to transform your board officers into change champions. You can share pertinent articles and book excerpts that build an appetite for rethinking the board's leadership role and process. You or a trusted consultant can give a presentation on the subject at an executive committee meeting. You also can promote attendance at national or regional board development workshops. Before you send board members to any kind of educational workshop, however, be sure that the message being delivered actually supports where you want the board to go. The world is filled with education and training that promotes the old-time passive–reactive model of board leadership.

If you have a generally supportive board chair, convince him or her to adopt board leadership design as a personal initiative and to sell the idea to other executive committee members. If your board chair is neutral and unwilling to go out on the limb for the design idea, you will have more difficulty turning other officers into champions of change. And if your board chair opposes the idea, it's best to put the design process on the back burner until a new chair takes office.

3. Emphasize the practical benefits to all board members. In selling the idea of a board design work session to other board members, the change champions should focus on the concrete benefits that will accrue to everyone involved. Few board members are likely to be moved by the idea of change for its own sake or of being on the cutting edge of the field of governance. What will move them is the notion that whatever resources they bring to the board room will be

fully used in making decisions that truly shape and guide the association. It does matter that the work of the board can become more important, interesting, and enjoyable, and that by participating in it one can become more skilled in governing—a prized skill that can be applied in other organizations. Many board members find the notion "Be all that you can—and want to—be as a board" quite appealing.

4. Few people welcome being informed of their weaknesses and offered an opportunity to correct them. You will want your board champions to sell the idea of a design work session not as a remedy for an underperforming board, but as an avenue to the next plateau of governance. I have never encountered a board that was not trying hard to provide direction, or that was not doing some things pretty well, even if it was just conscientiously reviewing finished budget requests and other documents. So, it normally does not stretch the truth to describe the process as "making a good board better," and it certainly sounds more appealing. You will also want your change champions to make the point that designing your own board is very different from being trained into being a better board. Most board members do not think of themselves as needing to be trained, and they have typically been exposed to enough poorly conceived and ineptly delivered training to avoid it like the plague.

5. Build wider ownership. The sooner you can expand ownership of the board design work session beyond the original change champions, the better your chances of having the session in the near future. One sure-fire way to build ownership is to involve board members in planning the session. (At least give them an opportunity to review and comment on the agenda before it's finalized.) Another strategy is to involve as large and diverse a group of board members as possible in playing formal leadership roles during the session. People who are busy leading do not have the time or inclination to sit back, with arms folded, and criticize the process.

6. Go ahead with less than 100-percent backing. Once you have a group of champions committed to conducting a board design session, schedule the event, without taking a formal vote of the whole board or attempting to clear everyone's schedules. To give everyone the opportunity to attend, put the retreat on the calendar at least three or four months in advance. Although you will want a majority of the board to participate in the retreat, recognize that the chance of getting

100-percent participation is quite slim. And more often than not, skeptical board members will participate once they see that it will be a well-designed, high-stakes session.

An Effective Design Retreat

To produce a board design that will stand the test of time, schedule an intensive work session or retreat that lasts at least one full day. Board members will need that time to work through the different pieces of the design and to make sure the design is technically workable as well as tailored to the unique needs and circumstances of your association.

They also will need time to build the kind of ownership on which implementation depends. Only when people participate in-depth in creating a role, structure, or process do they feel like owners of that creation.

A poorly designed and executed board retreat can set back the cause of board capacity building and design, leaving you worse off than if you had not done anything at all. And a failed retreat tends to leave a bad taste that doesn't go away quickly. Almost any board member you ask will recount a horror story about the retreat that bored them to death, or deteriorated into a screaming match midway through, or wasted a half-day crafting a one-paragraph mission statement. To ensure your retreat will be a productive and positive experience, you and your board change champions should take the following steps:

- Appoint an ad hoc board committee to plan the design retreat. Membership should include you, the board chair and officers, and perhaps other board members, but no more than one-quarter of the board. The committee's job is to fashion a clear set of objectives for the design retreat, determine the structure, and work out a detailed agenda.

- Set aside at least a day for the retreat. You cannot hope to develop even a rough draft of a board governance design in less than a day. Don't get trapped into agreeing to hold a three-hour meeting rather than a serious eight- to ten-hour retreat. What you might cover in two or three hours are contemporary trends in board leadership and the methodology the upcoming retreat will employ; this serves as a useful prelude to the full-fledged design retreat.

- Make sure that the meeting is highly participatory. Use breakout groups led by board members to expand board ownership of the event, sustain participants' interest, and generate more information than would be possible in plenary session. One national association's board, for example, employed six breakout groups to fashion different elements of the board leadership design. Three groups looked at the board's desired impacts in three governance areas (planning, operational oversight, and external/legislative relations), and three groups focused on the board itself (desired attributes and qualifications of members, desired performance of board members, and the desired board culture).

• Hold the design retreat in a comfortable location well away from the association's offices. This helps keep participants' minds away from business-as-usual concerns.

• Send all participants a detailed description of the retreat well in advance. Spell out the objectives, structure, and agenda, to allay any apprehension and to stimulate participation. Invited participants have been known to change their plans in order to attend a design retreat, based on seeing an impressive retreat description (called the "I can't afford to miss this" phenomenon).

• Use a professional facilitator with substantial experience in governing board design to help plan, facilitate, and follow up on the design retreat. Make sure the facilitator has done similar jobs successfully and she or he shares your and your board champions' commitment to the new model of board leadership. A well-qualified outside facilitator will bring objectivity and legitimacy to the process.

• Avoid using any formal consensus or decision-making techniques. By taking a brainstorming approach to the leadership design process, with no rank ordering or selection of right and wrong answers, participants can think freely. They don't have to worry about coming up with definitive answers to complex questions.

Build into the retreat a follow-up process that includes finalizing the various elements of the board design. One approach is to require that the professional facilitator prepare a set of action recommendations based on the retreat deliberations, which the board will review and act on subsequent to the retreat.

Many boards have successfully used an ad hoc governance steering committee or the executive committee to do the follow-up work of refining the design, developing an implementation schedule, and recommending final action to the full board. In some cases, a bylaws revision may be needed.

- Invite senior staff to participate. The design retreat offers an excellent executive development opportunity, since senior staff will help the board put new functions, structure, and process into operation. They can bring useful ideas to the design process, and working with board members in this kind of intensive session builds mutual understanding and respect.

Five Elements of Board Governance

Here are the major elements of a board governance design.

1. Board leadership vision. This element sets the board's sights broadly, in terms of its role and desired impacts. Going through the visioning process in a retreat setting can be a powerful self-educational tool, one that forces board members to focus on the level at which they intend to exercise leadership.

The vision provides a strategic framework within which board members can take the next design step—fashioning a more detailed leadership mission. Once the leadership vision has been formally adopted, it can be used to attract new board members and to build a more unified board.

A Clear Vision

The Council of Insurance Agents and Brokers (CIAB) formulated this board leadership vision:

If it is to provide the strong leadership that CIAB's basic health and future growth demand, the board's leadership vision should comprise the following:

- Serving as the steward and guardian of CIAB's values, vision, and mission.

- Providing strong strategic and policy direction for CIAB.

- Taking a leading, proactive role in planning and decision making.

- Serving as the preeminent driver of CIAB's growth and development.

- Monitoring CIAB's overall performance against clearly defined strategies and goals.

- Ensuring that all board members are fully engaged in the governance process and that the resources they bring to the board are fully utilized.

- Making sure that the board's composition is diverse enough to support a truly powerful strategic decision-making process and to facilitate external partnership building.

- Taking accountability for its own performance as CIAB's governing body.

2. Board governance mission. This second element moves into operational detail by identifying the major governance products that the board should devote significant time to producing—not alone, of course, but in active partnership with the CEO and management team. It tells where the board intends to direct its time and attention, not how it will carry out its responsibilities.

3. Board structure. The preeminent structural question is whether to have standing committees do the detailed governing work of the board and, if so, which ones. Standing committees have the advantage of enabling board members to delve into their governing work in greater depth than plenary board sessions allow and to develop valuable expertise. They tend to produce more ownership and satisfaction among board members, perhaps because volunteers can ask probing questions of association staff without the drama of a full board meeting. In addition, standing committees provide a venue for more relaxed and in-depth interaction between board and staff.

Many association boards in the past have found standing committees to be relatively unproductive vehicles for governing, because they have been organized not by broad governing streams but, rather, by narrow administrative functions, such as finance and personnel, and by programs and services, such as education, membership services, and the annual conference. Committees organized by particular programs and services and by narrow administrative functions inevitably fall victim to what I call the "tip of the administrative and program iceberg" effect. Board members' perspectives are narrowed by this kind of structure, allowing any particular

Time Well Spent

These examples of board governance missions resulted from real-life board design processes.

In the planning stream:
- Updated association values, vision, and mission
- Strategic issues deserving near-term attention
- Major innovation and change initiatives
- Annual operational priorities
- Annual program/function operational objectives
- Annual budget

In the operational oversight stream:
- Regular monitoring of program/financial performance
- Evaluation of program/service effectiveness
- Customer satisfaction surveys
- CEO performance evaluation
- External audit review and response
- Internal operating policies

In the external relations stream:
- Image determination and enhancement
- Public relations goals
- Stakeholder relationship goals
- Legislative relationship goals
- Positions on prospective legislation
- Revenue diversification strategies

A Strong Structure

Well-designed standing committees that are truly productive:

- Correspond to the broad governance functions or streams and cut across all association operations.
- Determine the full board agenda and serve as the major conduits to the board.
- Are composed only of board members, who serve on only one committee.
- Are strongly supported by the CEO and management team.

committee to see only a piece of the association, rather than the whole. And the content of their work has more to do with providing technical advice than actually governing. Such a poor design structure can do great damage over time. Not only does it weaken the board as a governing body, turning it instead into more of a grand technical advisory committee and robbing the association of seriously needed governance, but it also invites board meddling into administrative and program operations and hence promotes constant board–staff tension.

In response, many association boards have moved to a structure that organizes the board by its major governance functions, each of which cuts across the whole association: planning, operational oversight, and external relations. The board's planning committee, for example, works with the CEO to determine how board members will participate in the strategic and operational planning process of the association, develops and hosts major planning sessions involving the board (such as an annual strategic planning retreat), and refines and recommends the adoption of key planning products (such as the updated vision and mission statements).

The board's operational oversight committee would be responsible for reviewing and reporting to the full board on association program and financial performance, reviewing and developing responses to annual external audit reports, monitoring member/customer satisfaction, evaluating long-term program effectiveness, overseeing major internal administrative system enhancements, and reviewing and recommending adoption of major operational policies.

The board's external relations and volunteer involvement committee fashions strategies to strengthen the association's image and maintain relationships with key stakeholders, monitors volunteer involvement mechanisms and develops strategies to enhance such involvement, reviews and recommends marketing strategies, and develops and recommends adoption of association positions on legislative issues.

Where does the board's executive committee fit into this structure of standing committees organized by broad governance functions? Traditionally, executive committees have earned a deserved sinister reputation for secretive, manipulative behavior, resulting from their operating as a petite board that prescreens everything going to the full board. A more useful and positive role for an executive committee is to serve as the standing committee on board operations. In this capacity, the executive committee coordinates the work of standing committees, develops and oversees implementation of a strategy and budget for board capacity building, fashions board member performance standards and monitors such performance, handles the recruitment of new board members, and conducts CEO evaluation.

To carry out this demanding role, the executive committee must consist of the chairs of the standing committees, as well as other board officers, and must focus on maintaining an effective committee structure. Coordination and facilitation is not the same as screening, which the executive committee should avoid. Standing committees should report directly to the full board, not through the executive committee.

To ensure that your board's standing committees are truly productive governance engines, establish as an iron-clad rule that items, whether they are for action or information, get on the full board agenda only through the standing committees. The sole exception is the CEO's report. Organize the board agenda by standing committees, and require that all reports and recommendations be made by committee chairs and members, not by staff. This empowerment will, over time, build the credibility of the standing committees while also stimulating interest and fostering feelings of ownership among board members. With strong standing committees that truly direct full board meetings, board members won't feel like an audience for finished staff work.

The rule that every board member is to serve on one (and only one) standing governance committee must be rigorously observed. To spread board members' time more thinly makes a mockery of governance and ensures that complex issues receive too little attention. On the other hand, exempting any board member from service on a standing committee sends the message that some board members are too important to have to participate seriously in governing the association.

Every association has a need for nongoverning committees and task forces to provide technical advice. In designing your governance structure, ensure that these groups are established and overseen by the standing committees and consist only of nonboard volunteers. When board members do not serve on nongoverning committees, they can devote more attention to the business of governing and lessen the risk of becoming burned out due to over-involvement. Plus, this arrangement expands opportunities for nonboard volunteer involvement in the association.

4. Board human resource development. Boards, like any other organization, are basically people, and how well your board handles developing itself as a human resource will powerfully influence the effectiveness of its leadership. There are two major ways that your board can develop itself as a human resource: through the process of renewing board composition and through a formal program to build board member governing skills. The indispensable first step is to assign the responsibility for board development to a particular committee; the executive committee is often a good choice.

Executive committees of many associations have thought through the issue of board composition and have identified opportunities to diversify membership in the interest of stronger leadership. In this regard, many associations have recognized that limiting board membership to association members involved in the industry or profession that the association represents doesn't make sense in a rapidly changing, challenging world that demands strong and creative board leadership. Wider experience and more diverse perspectives are essential for creative leadership, and so diversity is a precious asset. Many association boards have also come to understand that treating board membership as the highest rung of the volunteer career ladder—as a kind of reward for active volunteer service—really misses the point, since in-depth technical expertise in the industry or profession isn't a serious requirement for good governance. Nor does volunteering in nongovernance roles really prepare anyone to govern. At the most, such active volunteering is a way of demonstrating commitment and skills in organizing, doing jobs, and working with people.

To gain the wide experience and diverse perspectives that strong governance demands these days, many association boards have reserved some slots (usually no more than 20 percent of the board) for "outside" board members—people from academe, related associations, or professions such as law and consulting. In addition, many executive committees are paying close attention to gender and racial diversity in determining the desired board composition. A more diverse board means not only a smarter board but also one with greater access to partnerships and financial resources.

It can be helpful for the executive committee to develop a profile of board membership attributes and qualifications, which is reviewed and adopted by the full board. For example, the Health Industry Distributors Association has identified desirable characteristics, such as "outspoken," "committed," "possessing connections with other associations," "being a critical thinker," "being open to change and understanding how to manage change," and "being at a senior level in member companies."

Using the profile as a guide, executive committees can play an active role in identifying and recruiting candidates to fill board seats. They may provide the profile to appointing or electing bodies, request recommendations based on the profile, interview potential candidates, and even check references.

Valuable Staff Assistance

Board standing committees cannot operate successfully on their own. As the CEO, you will want to make sure that these committees of volunteers receive strong staff support.

- Designate a member of your management team to serve as the liaison to each committee. The staff person should work closely with the committee chair to develop agendas and prepare for meetings.

- Assign to each staff liaison some other staff members to serve as a committee support team (assuming that you have a large enough staff).

- Make sure the management team regularly devotes significant time—collectively—to planning for, supporting, and monitoring the effectiveness of the standing committees.

Whatever method used to appoint board members—whether your board is self-appointing, is elected by the membership at an annual meeting, is appointed by one or more third parties, or some other method—your executive committee can and should play an active role in upgrading membership, because people are almost the whole ball game in the world of leadership. No structure or process, no matter how well designed, can make up for the wrong board composition. At the very least, the executive committee can make the profile of attributes and qualifications available to third-party electing or appointing bodies, so that they are aware of what your board considers its human resource requirements. Moving away from relying on the volunteer career-ladder approach and taking even the simplest steps to upgrade your board as a human resource will pay tremendous dividends.

Most boards do not pay systematic or close attention to developing their governance capacity, which is ironic, considering that your board is your association's preeminent leadership body. Apparently, we just haven't been in the habit of thinking about our boards as truly precious assets that demand development if they are to yield a powerful return to our associations. Your board can move well down the field by taking two simple steps: assigning the executive committee or some other standing committee responsibility for board capacity building; and charging that committee to develop an annual capacity-building program, along with a budget to support it. The capacity-building programs of association boards that I have worked with include some of the following elements:

- Holding an annual work session during which the board assesses its performance, identifies and analyzes shortfalls, and adopts enhancements in board processes and structure.
- Sending selected board members to pertinent training programs on governance education.
- Developing and administering an orientation program for new board members that concentrates on the role, functions, structure, and performance standards of the board itself, rather than focusing solely on association programs.
- Building a library of governance books and periodicals and regularly circulating items of special interest to board members.

5. Board performance management. To take accountability for its own performance as the association's governing body, the board must set clear performance standards for itself and for individual members. As the CEO, you have a large stake in your board's taking accountability for its own performance. Not only will it result in needed leadership, but it also will provide you with greater security. Remember: Boards frustrated by their own boring and unproductive work have a tendency not to blame themselves but to point their fingers at the CEO.

Of course, it's not worth the time or trouble to develop performance standards unless they are actually put into practice. Perhaps the most important step your association can take in this regard is to assign responsibility for monitoring the board's overall performance to a standing committee, such as the executive committee.

Assessing individual board member performance, however, gets into sensitive territory. The association boards that have been successful here have taken a fairly low-key, positive, nonpunitive approach. They typically ask chairs of standing committees to identify serious shortfalls (such as missing several consecutive meetings) and to contact the erring board member to identify the problem and help remedy it. Only in the most extreme cases is removal from the board recommended.

The great thing about standard setting by and for conscientious, high-achieving people, such as your average board member, is that they invariably rise to the occasion, hitting the mark set because that is their approach to life. Standards tend to be self-fulfilling and require virtually no enforcement. Performance

Great Performances

The board performance standards can grow out of the vision and mission statements formulated during the board design retreat. Other standards, which can be developed at a retreat and refined later, might govern interaction among board members. For instance, the American Health Information Management Association developed these rules:

- Be open minded
- Be respectful of each other
- Don't have a personal agenda
- Keep the interest of the whole association at the forefront
- Be ethical

The Council of Insurance Agents and Brokers (CIAB) expects individual board members to satisfy these standards in their work on the board:

- Attend full board and committee meetings
- Be well prepared for meetings
- Participate
- Meet deadlines
- Consistently support the CIAB mission
- Stress member recruitment
- Speak on behalf of CIAB—at the lectern and before legislative committees
- Help improve communication with the membership

standards also can be used when recruiting for board vacancies. Standards clarify for prospective board members what's involved in serving on your board. They also send a clear message to all candidates: "This is not your everyday, ho-hum board; we demand top performance, and we're truly worthy of your commitment of time and energy."

Maintaining a Healthy Partnership

Philosophy and attitude count tremendously in the business of building and maintaining a strong, positive relationship with your board. The odds that you will succeed in developing and keeping intact a close, mutually satisfying, productive working partnership with your board will improve greatly if you believe that:

- Your board is a precious resource to your association that must be fully deployed in leading the association (rather than thinking that your role is to protect your staff from board incursions).
- Your board should follow the more contemporary model of strong, proactive leadership in setting association directions and making strategic decisions (rather than being a traditional passive–reactive board).
- You should play an active, facilitative role in helping your board develop a governance design that clearly defines the products and outcomes it will devote time to producing and the structure and process it will follow in carrying out its governance work.

Easier said than done, obviously. I must warn you to be on guard for the possibility that you will make an intellectual commitment to these beliefs, while at an emotional level—in your heart of hearts—you feel too distrustful and fearful to serve in the board capacity-building role with the intensity and enthusiasm it demands. Many of your board members are likely to have little understanding of or appetite for building governance capacity. Bringing them around to a more modern view and getting them committed to the design process will demand that you be committed, courageous—dealing with your own fear of losing control—and persistent.

As you work with your board to fully develop its leadership capacity, here's how you can strengthen the partnership.

Make the board–CEO relationship a high priority. Lots of your prime time and attention: That's the recipe for keeping your relationship with your board healthy. That means spending between 20 percent and 25 percent of your time—when you are not exhausted and are still mentally alert—thinking about your board and how it is doing, diagnosing your board's developmental needs, and strategizing how to help your board take certain capacity-building steps.

One association CEO takes a couple of hours every Sunday morning in her study, armed with a blank legal pad, to think about her relationship with the board and what steps she needs to take during the coming weeks. She has made a real, not just rhetorical, commitment to the partnership.

Be honest, open, and flexible in dealings with your board. You may not always reveal your whole hand to your board—at least not to the full board, say, when you are working to secure your board's commitment to participate in a governance design retreat. But never intentionally mislead board members, hide bad news from them, or load them down with so much paper that they can't really tell how well certain programs are performing. By being honest and open, you will build a line of credit with your board that can help you get through the inevitable rough times.

Being flexible means that you are willing to adjust your partnership with your board—short of doing something that truly violates principle—to account for its members' changing needs and desires. Don't stand on principle when principle is not really at issue.

For example, let's say that your association is moving to a new headquarters. This involves substantial cost, as well as a new image that you and the board have agreed to promote. Your board's operational oversight committee has expressed interest in being involved in the design of the headquarters, which strictly speaking, falls in the administrative bailiwick. But you understand the committee's need for input and see no principle seriously in danger of being violated, so you support and facilitate the committee's detailed involvement. By contrast, if a board member begins to call one of your senior staff members frequently with time-consuming requests, a principle is, indeed, involved, and you must not allow the situation to continue. *Update the board on CEO leadership requirements and expectations.* If some time has passed since you took the CEO reins, the association's situation and the board membership may have changed significantly. Perhaps the majority that hired you has faded away, along with the

CEO Responsibilities in Detail

Your detailed position description should cover the following key areas of chief executive performance:

- **Support for your board,** including playing an active role in supporting the board's standing committees and helping the board develop its leadership capacity.

- **External relations,** including speaking on behalf of your association in public forums and maintaining key external relationships.

- **Strategic planning** and entrepreneurial development, making sure that your association's strategic planning process is focused on innovation and action. The process should involve board and staff members fully and creatively, focusing on opportunities to grow and to diversify programs and services.

- **Administrative management,** making sure the day-to-day systems and operations of your association run effectively and efficiently.

- **Your leadership style,** describing how the board expects you to carry out the foregoing responsibilities in the interest of promoting a particular kind of internal culture (for example, helping people to feel secure).

priorities for executive leadership that existed at the time. To ensure that your relationship with the board continues to be positive, renegotiate CEO leadership expectations regularly and formally. Otherwise, you may find yourself held accountable for not performing a function well that you were not even aware you should be performing.

CEO leadership expectations are negotiated with your board at two levels:

- CEO board functions and responsibilities are described in the CEO position description.
- Specific CEO performance targets—within the framework of the position description—are negotiated annually with your board.

In these times of rapid change, it is wise to pull your position description out of the files at least every two or three years, take a crack at updating it, and then discuss it in detail with the appropriate board standing committee. (I strongly recommend that your board's executive committee play this role.) Of course, you may not even have a detailed job description to start with; if so, put developing a complete one at the top of your board to-do list.

Updating the CEO position description offers the occasion to consider your board's highest priority concerns relative to your leadership. By contrast, an annual executive committee–CEO negotiation session on specific performance targets establishes standards to use in CEO evaluation. This session should be held at the end of the fiscal year—after next year's operational plan and budget have been adopted. The focus should be on CEO performance targets above and beyond the association-wide targets built into the operational plan and budget. As the CEO, you are obviously accountable for achievement of programmatic and financial targets. Beyond that, you are accountable *individually* for certain targets.

For example, you and your board might agree that you will spend at least one-third of your time during the next fiscal year exploring a merger with two other associations in the same industry. Or you may devote significant time to implementing new board standing committees or spend a quarter of your time out on the hustings raising the profile of the association around the country. These kinds of commitments—which are important and certainly the business of your board—would never surface through the association's planning process.

Ensure that you are regularly, formally, and systematically evaluated by your board. Spending time to negotiate CEO performance standards and targets with your board pays off when your performance is evaluated annually, preferably with the board's executive committee. Even though CEO evaluation is commonly touted as one of a board's preeminent responsibilities, many boards fail to do it well or avoid it entirely. Board members often shy away from the CEO evaluation because being critical is just plain unpleasant, at least when it happens face-to-face.

You, as the CEO, cannot afford to let this happen. A serious, in-depth, annual evaluation is essential to maintaining your working partnership with your board—and probably the most powerful guarantee of occupational security. Without an annual, formal look at your performance, serious questions may not

In It Together

The chance of building a mutually satisfying relationship will be greater if, as part of a board governance design process, all board members agree to and formalize the following basic principles:

- The board chair is a volunteer who is basically accountable for leading the board; the CEO is a professional on staff responsible for running all association affairs on a day-to-day basis.
- The board chair and the CEO share responsibility for maintaining relationships with association members, key stakeholders, and the wider public, and they must work through a sensible division of labor in this area.
- The CEO takes direction only from the board as a whole, never from the board chair individually.
- The CEO evaluation should be performed by a board committee, not by the board chair as an individual.

surface and may remain underground and allowed to fester. Countless CEOs have lost their jobs because of performance problems that weren't articulated until their relationship with their boards had frayed beyond repair.

You can help your board evaluate your performance by helping it develop a formal process. It should involve these elements:

- A standing committee that takes responsibility for negotiating CEO performance targets and conducting the annual evaluation. (The executive committee is ideally suited for this role.)
- At least a half-day devoted to evaluation, in a meeting with the CEO present. (A subcommittee of the executive committee might prepare a preliminary assessment to serve as a starting point.)
- Measurement of performance against the targets that were negotiated a year earlier—not using a meaningless checklist that is sometimes employed to save time and avoid serious thinking.
- Detailed dialogue between committee members and the CEO, aimed at bringing issues to the surface and working through strategies to correct performance problems.
- Generation of a written evaluation document that clearly and in detail identifies performance shortfalls and confirms corrective actions.

Since CEO evaluation is a board responsibility, any interested board members should be invited to sit in on the executive committee's evaluation session, and all board members should receive the written evaluation document. CEO evaluation should never be delegated to the board chair alone, nor should it be done informally or kept secret from any board members.

Work as a team with your board chair. Savvy CEOs pay lots of attention to building a close, positive partnership with their board chair. A good relationship with the entire board is much easier to maintain if the CEO and board chair work as a team.

It is incumbent on you, as the CEO, to take the initiative in building a solid relationship with your chair. Understand what makes the board chair tick, and respond to his or her expectations and needs to the extent feasible.

Like any human relationship, the board chair–CEO partnership will benefit from "quality time." Seek to understand what your board chair needs and wants from the leadership experience, and figure out how to work effectively with this particular person. Some chairs, for example, thrive on informal communication. Others work best when they are formally briefed in writing. Also look for every opportunity to make your board chair the owner of initiatives, such as undertaking a board governance design process. Your willingness to lead from behind, allowing your board chair to bask in the limelight, will help keep the relationship strong.

Building the Capacity To Lead and Manage Change

A KEY CHARACTERISTIC of associations that thrive and grow in times of rapid change is the capacity to lead and manage their own change. What will that change be like? That's the question that you, as the CEO, must face. Will you exert some control over that change, directing and guiding it in the interest of the association's health and growth? Or will you be changed—inevitably—by the forces of change in the wider world, becoming in a sense the victim of those forces?

Either way, your association will experience change in today's world; standing pat, safely observing from the sidelines, isn't a viable option. But if you want to have a significant say in the nature and pace of that change, ensuring that the costs and "pain" are contained and the benefits maximized, you'll have to invest heavily in the business of leading and managing it. Otherwise, the inevitable changes thrust upon your association are likely to be painful and expensive, if not lethal. They may include declining member numbers and revenues, loss of market share to one or more competitors, and growing frustration among volunteers over antiquated structures that chew up tremendous time without obvious benefit.

Your association's taking command of its own change is perhaps the most powerful defensive and offensive move it can make in this challenging world.

The CEO Challenge

As the CEO, you're the point person in building the association's capacity to lead and manage change. Playing this critical part of your leadership role will require you to take the lead in these areas:

- Putting in place a process that will enable your association to identify where changes are needed, to plan the changes, and to ensure that the planned changes are translated from words to action.

- Involving your board and staff in managing change, making sure that the association takes full advantage of their expertise, experience, and other resources while also building their ownership of the change process.

- Dealing with the natural resistance that people tend to feel toward change, especially when it directly affects their day-to-day affairs.

Not Just Any Change Will Do

We are not talking about change for change's sake. Obviously, poorly conceived and executed change causes harm, just as sensible and well-planned and implemented change produces benefit. Some key characteristics of good change are that it:

- Fits within the strategic framework of your association—its values, its vision for the future, and the mission that defines what the organization is all about now. Because the organizational values, vision, and mission should evolve over time as circumstances and association aspirations change, make sure your association periodically updates its strategic framework.

- Capitalizes on your association's strengths and opportunities to grow.

- Yields significant benefits to the association at a reasonable cost and at an acceptable level of risk.

- Is a chewable bite for your association—affordable technically, financially, and in terms of the board, volunteer, and staff time and energy required. It is all too easy to win a particular change battle at the price of disrupting association operations, demoralizing volunteers, and burning out an overextended staff.

These points about good change may strike you as being unscientific and unamenable to technology. Yet consider that each point involves making a human judgment, without any help from a computer. That's why it's important that your association's process for leading and managing change draws on a diverse mix of board members, other volunteers, staff, and perhaps even "outsiders." Each group brings different perspectives and judgments to the process.

You must guard against too much neatness and efficiency in the process, at the price of cutting off the kind of serious questioning, open brainstorming, and searching analysis that are essential for good judgment. Discipline and control come naturally and easily; while they are important allies, they can be stultifying if they're applied too soon in the change process.

Prepare yourself and your colleagues for the tension that comes with serious change efforts. Even thinking about the possibility of change, much less actually changing, can produce considerable anxiety. Know going into the change game that it's not going to be much, if any, fun for anybody involved.

A Tough Nut To Crack

Significant, planned, systematically implemented change is the exception to the rule—both for individuals and organizations. Why is change such a tough nut to crack?

- The constant pressure of day-to-day affairs can be demanding and even beguiling. Phone calls, e-mail, and faxes never stop coming, and crises are frequent visitors. If you're not careful in your personal life, you can find yourself devoting 110 percent of your time and energy to daily living. Organizations aren't any different—it's just harder to spot the phenomenon at work.

- The resources—time, money, energy, knowledge—that your association can bring to bear on change are finite and often limited. Rare is the association blessed with a flexible fund of $100,000 or more that is dedicated to financing innovation. Even harder to find is one that has capable staff with enough spare time to undertake the innovation challenge. The window for change is seldom open more than a mere crack, and may seem firmly shut much of the time in the real world.

- There is the inevitable human resistance to change, which is often so well hidden in the heads of resisters that they aren't even aware of resisting. Comfort with things the way they are is a powerful force and the prime cause of the inertia that slows or even blocks efforts to change. Sometimes resistance makes sense, certainly when a planned change is clearly going to do more harm than good (say, another one of those misunderstood and misapplied quick fixes like total quality management). But resistance also comes from an illogical, emotional wellspring, for example, fear of looking foolish or failing, which your conscious mind might not even recognize for what it is.

- Until recent years, long-range strategic planning has served more as a lengthening of operational planning rather than an innovative tool for leading change. In other words, five-year plans are often the annual operational plan times five.

Planning Myths and Realities

Almost all planning done by organizations focuses on controlling and managing *what is,* not on generating significant change. This is certainly true of operational planning and budgeting, but even so-called strategic planning has tended to confirm and project into the future for some arbitrary period—typically, three or five years—what an organization already is doing.

Traditionally, strategic planning has involved two scenarios. In the first, a three- or five-year plan (or set of goals) serves as an umbrella within which the annual plan is developed. In the second scenario, every program or function of your association fashions a long-range plan, and all of these are combined into a master plan for the association. Either way, such long-range plans are typically put away before you start developing your annual plan and budget; any connections between the two are superficial at best.

It is also important to acknowledge both the power and the limitations of that tried-and-true tool—the Mississippi River of planning—the annual operational plan and budget. What it does—efficiently and effectively—is update, refine, adjust, embellish, and allocate resources to what your association is already doing. This is a critical task, because your association's current operations probably consume 95 percent or more of its resources. What the annual operational planning and budgeting process cannot do—even when it is extended for three or five years into the future—is accomplish significant innovation for your association.

In real life, individuals and organizations produce serious change when they plan and manage in two parallel streams:

- **Running the shop** includes operational planning, budget preparation, and other control techniques, such as financial reporting and management team meetings.

- **Changing and growing the shop** involves essentially different planning techniques and survives only when it is kept separate from day-to-day affairs.

If the two streams intermingle, the day-to-day concerns inevitably overwhelm innovation and change. To prevent that from happening, approach the challenge of change in this way:

What my association is already doing, it's doing. Let's put it aside for the moment, and ask: Beyond what it's already engaged in, which is enshrined in the annual operational plan and budget in great detail, what should my association do that's new and different and that isn't likely to be accomplished through business as usual?

If the changes I need to make relate to refining and updating what I am already doing, then I can rely on my tried-and-true operational planning and budgeting process. But if the change challenges are complex and require new responses, I must turn to a different, completely separate process to get this innovation job done.

In other words, I must move to a new game, with different rules, that explicitly focuses on significant change.

The Strategic Change Portfolio

Long-range or strategic planning basically has been an operational tool that has had little to do with serious innovation. In light of the rate and depth of the changes in the world these days, however, projecting current programs and services into the future much beyond a year can be a waste of time.

Fortunately, you can put a practical, affordable, and powerful planning tool to work in your association to lead and manage change: the strategic change portfolio. Its underlying premise is that both you and your association must break away from the notion that operational and strategic planning can be methodically linked in an elaborate, integrated system.

Think of your association's strategic change portfolio as an investment portfolio, where you keep and manage your change projects (strategic change initiatives) rather than stocks and bonds. By keeping your association's strategic change initiatives in one place and carrying them out through a separate process and structure, you ensure that they receive enough attention and don't get buried in the pressures and crises of the association's day-to-day operations.

The strategic change initiatives within your association's strategic change portfolio are essentially projects that are intended to address major "change challenges"—problems, barriers, and opportunities that are high-stakes enough to put in the portfolio. Each initiative consists of:

- A clear target or outcome (for example, We will launch a new membership campaign by September 1. We will accomplish a merger with XYZ Association within fifteen months. We will put new board committees and a more effective leadership process in place by June 30).

- An action plan that spells out the steps that must be taken to hit the target, along with deadlines and accountabilities.

- The project budget, which identifies the resources required to implement the initiative and where they will come from.

You, along with your board, staff, and volunteers, are undoubtedly adept at project planning; that is not where the power of the strategic investment portfolio lies. What makes the portfolio a unique change vehicle is its explicit tie to your association's strategic framework: the values that guide you and the vision to which you aspire. It focuses on addressing specific change challenges to move toward your vision, to more fully realize your values in practice, and to deal with problems and barriers that keep you from fulfilling your vision or putting your values into practice.

Without the framework of clearly defined values and an overarching vision, your association's change efforts are apt to produce as much harm as good. Values provide the boundaries beyond which your association won't go. For example, the value "we believe in a humane environment in which staff are treated with respect and consideration" would stay the hand that is tempted to load more strategic change initiatives on staff than they can possibly handle while still running the shop.

Vision provides the overall ends and purposes toward which any changes must move and makes it possible to choose which change challenges your association should tackle during any given year. Vision helps you, your board, and staff to answer *why* your association should make changes; values tell you *how* you should change.

The strategic change portfolio is a realistic tool to use in changing and growing because of its selectivity. This characteristic saves your association from making unrealistic wish lists or from becoming dangerously overextended. The rule is clear: Your association's strategic change portfolio should consist only of projects that you can realistically expect to carry out, without stretching your association too thin. The point is not to shoot high in hopes of hitting a few targets; it is to focus on several important targets and make sure you achieve them—on time and within budget.

The Old and the New

The strategic change portfolio differs in several ways from traditional five-year planning. For instance, each strategic change initiative in your association's portfolio has a different time frame: This one's to be accomplished in eight months, that one in three years, and that other one in fifteen months. As strategic change initiatives are achieved (the board committees are now functioning; the new membership program has been launched), they drop out of the portfolio and others are added.

This isn't as neat a package as the old-time five-year strategic plan—but it reflects life in the fast lane. It's manageable, however, because you make it a formal part of the annual planning cycle and also rigorously segregate it from all other association operations. The strategic change initiatives that make up the portfolio are generated by

a well-defined component of your association's planning process and are never allowed to become buried in all of the details of running the association. Consequently, you can't lose track of them.

It doesn't take an inordinate amount of discipline to set aside particular hours on particular days to manage the strategic change portfolio. Today, for example, at 3 p.m., the task force fashioning one strategic change initiative—the merger with another association—will meet; tomorrow at 9 a.m., our management team, meeting as the strategic steering committee, will review progress in implementing the four strategic change initiatives currently in the portfolio. And, by the way, on Wednesday at 2 p.m., the management team will hold its weekly operational update meeting.

Your Board's Involvement

Fashioning or updating your association's strategic change portfolio involves the following key steps:

- Updating your association's strategic framework: its values, vision, and mission.
- Identifying and selecting the change challenges you intend to address during the coming year.
- Fashioning the strategic change initiatives to address the selected change challenges.

Many associations employ an annual board–CEO–management team strategic work session (or retreat) early in the planning cycle (say, in March for an association whose fiscal year begins on January 1) to update their strategic framework and to identify change challenges. Such a retreat can also be used to produce guidance for the normal operational planning and budget preparation process that begins in the spring or early summer (e.g., a set of operational planning priorities). Following the retreat, two streams of planning move forward concurrently—in parallel—and are kept separate, even though the same cast of characters—wearing different "hats"—leads and manages both streams:

- The process of selecting the change challenges and fashioning the strategic change initiatives, which is often accomplished by staff and/or volunteer task forces working closely with the board's planning committee.
- The normal operational plan/budget preparation via the association's functional and program units.

The annual strategic work session that kicks off both planning streams is an ideal place for your board to participate in your association's planning in a proactive, creative fashion that takes full advantage of your board as a strategic resource for your association. There can be no question that the work is of critical importance. How can anything outrank in potential impact and complexity updating your association's values, vision, and mission and identifying the change challenges that your association might tackle over the coming year? Your board is uniquely qualified for this kind of task this early in the planning cycle, which benefits from diverse experiences, talents, and perspectives. And your board will love actually dealing with the truly big questions and deliberating on association directions, rather than passively thumbing through a finished document at the tail end of the planning process.

In an intensive one- to two-day work session, your board cannot reasonably expect to go much further than getting a preliminary grasp of the key change challenges and exploring possible strategic change initiatives. The process of selecting the challenges to be addressed, much less fashioning the initiatives to address them, deserves more time and attention subsequent to the work session. A typical scenario is for the management team to massage the change challenges in a follow-up work session, reach consensus on the ones to be tackled during the coming year, and recommend their selection to the board's planning committee. Once the planning committee has agreed, staff and/or volunteer task forces can commence with developing strategic change initiatives.

The Strategic Framework

Although updating your association's values, vision, and mission is a strategic, high-impact activity, quite often it is totally ignored, or it is treated in a perfunctory fashion. This happens for three reasons:

- Associations sometimes feel so pressured by the demands of day-to-day events that pausing for any significant amount of time to focus on more fundamental questions seems like a luxury that they can ill afford.

- Associations take what I call the "pithy paragraph" approach to values, vision, and mission. This approach treats these precious products as general guidance for the association that is intended to inform the wider public and to inspire staff and volunteers, but not to serve as a truly powerful driver of significant association change.

- The discomfort that comes from examining fundamental principles and purposes in any depth can cause people to shy away from spending much time thinking about values, vision, and mission. After all, this is where we challenge what is and open up the Pandora's Box of what might be, which can be pretty frightening for both individuals and organizations.

Whatever the reasons, you must make sure that your board and management team are intensively involved in updating your association's values, vision, and mission if you want your association's change to produce powerful, positive results. Far from being merely a perfunctory frontispiece to the change process, your association's values, vision, and mission make it possible for you to select your change challenges rationally and hence to ensure that you invest your organization's finite and precious resources wisely in pursuing change. Without this strategic framework as a serious guide in your planning, you are apt to fall victim to preconceived notions in selecting change challenges and fashioning initiatives, and your association is just as apt to produce bad change as good.

Values and vision create the gap between your association's current situation (programs/services/resources/capabilities) and your association's ultimate aspirations. Values and vision give direction to your association's change investments; they point your strategic change initiatives toward long-range ends, rather than merely reacting to the crises and pressures of the moment. Values bring in ethical concerns and boundaries of conduct, while the mission forces you to think twice before moving beyond the current definition of your association.

There is no one strategic framework for all times and places. As the circumstances in which your association functions change (member needs and expectations, the structure of the industry or profession, emerging technologies, and so forth) along with your association's self-knowledge and its capacities, then your strategic framework will also evolve. Your vision of what the association needs and wants to be and do will inevitably expand; over time, this will expand your basic definition of the business your association is in: its mission.

Your association's strategic framework is perhaps your strongest ally in building loyalty, commitment, and unity among your board and staff members—and you'll need those in abundance as you move through the change process. People are more likely to bear the burden of change when they understand and are inspired by ultimate ends and broad purposes. That's why your board and management team should revisit the values, vision, and mission annually in an intensive work session—not just review the previous year's statement. Remember: New board members who did not participate in last year's session will not own what they have not helped to create. Their participation will help ensure that you have a relevant, living, breathing strategic framework that your board actually uses in leading change.

Here's a more detailed look at each element of the strategic framework:

Values: our golden rules. Your association's values are its most cherished beliefs and principles. They tell you, your board, and staff what your association should be like inside (the conditions people work in and the rules for working together that make up your culture) and what rules govern how you carry out your operations.

A carefully crafted values statement can foster loyalty and commitment and build unity—but only if it is taken seriously and not tucked into a three-ring binder and forgotten. Taking your values seriously means keeping them on your association's front burner—for example, by bringing them into your annual strategic work session—and dealing with obvious gaps between stated values and actual practice. Ignoring values gaps is a sure way to erode credibility and commitment among board and staff members.

Inconsistencies and conflicts are inevitable in the realm of values. A common conflict is the belief in member services of the highest quality versus the value of cost consciousness and prudent financial management. One of the association board's most important functions is to reconcile such value conflicts through the planning process. One approach is to bring the values into your annual strategic work session and ask all participants to refer to them during your deliberations. Identify and examine any notable gaps between values and practice—they are potential change challenges. Any contradictory values should be noted and discussed in detail.

Vision: our desired long-term future. Your association's vision is a picture of its desired impacts on members; on the industry or profession; and on its wider environment in terms of role, scope, and size. Think of a canvas that you, your board, and your management team, perhaps along with other volunteers and staff, must fill with as much detail as possible.

If you take the pithy paragraph approach—fashioning an elegant three- or four-sentence vision—you might produce something for public relations and marketing but nothing with value for leading change. Instead, approach the process of visioning with seriousness. Devote time and attention to identifying all of the important elements that make up your association vision, with enough detail to provide direction when it comes time to select change challenges.

Mission: defining what we are. Vision and mission are often thought of as being one and the same, but they are very different elements of your association's strategic framework. While your vision is a picture of what your association aspires to be and do over the long run—and is hence aspirational—your

---

We Believe in...

The Association for Investment Management and Research (AIMR) fashioned a values statement at a two-day retreat. It included the following elements:

- Ethical conduct, fairness, integrity
- Volunteerism/local and regional participation
- Free capital markets
- Full disclosure
- High-quality customer service
- Continuing education
- Consensus building through teamwork
- A multifaceted profession defined by a coherent, detailed body of knowledge
- A truly global profession
- The strength that comes from union, community, and cooperative effort

That Vision Thing

The following excerpt of a detailed vision statement is drawn from the Council of Insurance Agents and Brokers (CIAB).

- Expanded opportunities in our industry
- Attraction of new talent to the industry
- CIAB's being the preeminent insurance association
- A sounder, more positive regulatory environment
- A more positive public image for the insurance industry
- Widespread ethical conduct in the industry
- Enhanced professional standards in the industry
- Cultural diversity being widely promoted in the industry
- Industry firms being more competitive
- Expanded global opportunities for members
- Increased efficiency (lower unit costs) in the industry
- Effective defended producer interests
- Stronger company/intermediary relationships
- More effective utilization of technology in the industry
- CIAB's being recognized as the preeminent resource and spokesperson for the industry

mission is a description of your association now. It should address your association's members/customers, products and services, and basic "production" and service delivery mechanisms.

Stating your mission in a pithy paragraph or catchy slogan can be valuable for public relations and marketing, but for purposes of fashioning your strategic change portfolio, map out your association's mission in detail. This can be done in rough form at your annual strategic work session that kicks off the planning cycle and subsequently refined by the management team and board planning committee.

Your association's mission serves two basic purposes. First, it clarifies for the wider world what makes your association special and separates it from all other nonprofit organizations. Second, it provides you, your board, and your management team with a disciplinary device that keeps your association from willy-nilly diversification into new programs and services.

Think of your mission not so much as an inspirational or aspirational device, but as a brake in the change process. As your association's vision expands, pointing it toward new programs, functions, and customers, it puts pressure on your mission, which resists being expanded ("This is who we are, and those new things being considered are not"). This resistance—institutional second thoughts, if you will—keeps your association from being swept away by enthusiasm and spreading itself too thinly, perhaps even jeopardizing its core business in pursuit of tantalizing opportunities.

You should never forget as you help your board and management team grapple with vision and mission that, because they relate to the fundamental nature of your association, considering them produces considerable creative tension. Living through the tension— effectively balancing and reconciling the "competing" demands of vision and mission—will be a critical path to positive association change and growth, but that doesn't make the process any easier. You should expect to encounter a lot of resistance to the process of reconciling and balancing them. Anything that raises the specter of change will cause anxiety and tension, and so don't be surprised if many of your colleagues appear to prefer the perfunctory pithy paragraph approach. At least it doesn't rock the boat! But as the CEO, you must push for the kind of detailed examination that facilitates significant, positive change. Once again, this is why an intensive retreat setting is essential; to try to work through something this complex and anxiety inducing in a normal business setting is doomed to failure.

Identifying Change Challenges

Think of a change challenge as a very important issue in the form of an opportunity to move toward your association's vision, or a problem or barrier standing in the way of your association's progress toward its vision. A change challenge is essentially a question: "Should we respond to this issue by doing something new and different?"

Change challenges come in diverse forms. They generally relate to four areas:

- New programs and services that respond to members' new needs and demands. These are often tied to changes in the external

---

Mission Possible

Here's an example of a mission statement fleshed out in detail for planning (not public relations) purposes. It was developed by the Association of Investment Management and Research.

- Our key customers are our members, who can be divided into three groups: investment professionals, CFA charterholders, and CFA candidates.

- The products we produce for these member groups are:

  - For investment professionals: standards, seminars, education, a forum for communication with colleagues, certification, information.
  - For CFA charterholders: continuing education, CFA Body of Knowledge, research, standards of practice, maintenance of the integrity of the Charter and its enhancement.
  - For CFA candidates: study guides, preparation materials, the CFA examination, the CFA designation.

environment and growing and diversifying your association's membership. For example:

- The appearance of powerful new management information technologies that will make member companies more competitive—in the context of an increasingly competitive industry.
- Accelerating decline in membership that's connected to rapid consolidation in the industry your association represents.
- Demand for a new membership category in response to evolving markets.
- The opportunity to expand membership internationally in response to a growing demand for professional certification and educational programming in a rapidly developing profession.
- The need for more high-powered education and training aimed at building stronger boards.

• Member participation in your association's affairs. Examples include:

- Dramatically declining member time to devote to association business, especially when the volunteer involvement structure was designed in a different era (for example, a plethora of volunteer-driven committees and monthly luncheon meetings).
- A growing demand among volunteers for higher impact participation—more "bang for the buck" in volunteering.

• Association image and public relations. For example:

- Evidence that a substantial number of your association's members and key stakeholders view the association as a "good old boys" club that doesn't welcome or celebrate diversity.
- The growing importance of federal and state lobbying efforts in response to legislation affecting your members.

• Internal leadership and management. Examples include:

- An increasingly dysfunctional board that is frustrated about its passive–reactive role and has begun to nitpick the CEO's recommendations.
- An elaborate long-range planning process that requires an inordinate amount of time to produce pounds of paper but little serious innovation—in an environment demanding rapid, large-scale change.

– High staff turnover at the mid-management level that is disrupting programs and frustrating volunteers.

The annual strategic work session involving your association's board and management team is an excellent place to identify such change challenges and to gain a broad understanding of what lies behind them. It works well to use break-out groups that focus on three areas:

1. Scanning the external environment. Look at conditions and trends pertinent to your association's vision and mission; the industry or profession it serves; and the welfare of its members, including legislative, political, technological, social, and cultural factors.

2. Scanning association strengths and weaknesses in key resource areas, such as leadership and management capacity, image, and finances.

3. Examining association performance and identifying gaps between vision and actual accomplishments.

Taking a few hours to look at the internal and external environments in some detail probably will generate many more change challenges than can be dealt with in the coming year. New opportunities, needs, and demands will always overwhelm your association's resources, and so the critical challenge is to be selective in which ones to deal with.

In practice, you do not want to spend much time distinguishing between which change challenges are "operational" and which are truly "strategic" in a theoretical sense. Instead, you, your board, and your management team should identify for special attention (though perhaps not in the coming year) those change challenges that cannot be safely left to the normal operational planning and management processes. Perhaps they relate to high-stakes opportunities and costs (such as a dramatic membership decline or a large new revenue source), are too complex to manage in a business-as-usual fashion, or are high-level "orphans" that do not have a home within any association function, program, or administrative unit.

Deciding where a change challenge belongs—in the business-as-usual stream or in the strategic change portfolio—is not a matter of scientific logic; rather, it involves the judgment of your association's leadership—board, CEO, and management team—arrived at together, around the same table, with enough time to examine, question, and debate. This is why your annual strategic work session is an excellent venue for identifying and analyzing your change challenges. Also, this process is far better accomplished in a top-down fashion, since it requires environment-wide and organization-wide perspectives. The old-time approach of building strategy bottom-up was notorious for missing the really strategic change challenges while confirming the conventional wisdom. This does not mean, however, that you cannot program in widespread participation at all levels of your association in fashioning and implementing strategic change initiatives.

Making Your Selections

At any given time your association is probably using virtually every dollar, hour, and ounce of energy just to run its day-to-day affairs. That's why you can't tackle too many strategic change challenges concurrently. Your challenge—and the real magic of the process—is to involve your board and management team in choosing the right change challenges. The objective is to achieve the most favorable ratio of association benefit compared to the likely cost to the association of taking action on a change challenge.

Many associations have learned that the process of selecting change challenges works better if you ask this question: What will happen to our association if we do not take action on this change challenge during the coming year? The answer may be in terms of a lost opportunity. For example: If we don't apply for the grant funding now, we probably won't have the same opportunity in the foreseeable future. If we do not move to establish an international presence, another association will undoubtedly move to capture the potential international membership, which may be lost to us forever. If we do not pursue a merger with a sister association, it will probably seek another partner and leave us alone in an increasingly competitive environment.

The answer may be expressed in terms of the direct damage averted. For example: If we do not address the growing morale problem among our staff, we may lose some irreplaceable employees. If we do not act to deal with an increasingly frustrated board, we will find it extremely difficult to do strategic planning and policy making, and the CEO's position probably will be threatened. If we do not deal with an archaic volunteer structure that rewards "good old boys and girls" while chewing up volunteer time in wheel-spinning activity, we will most likely continue to lose members.

The change challenges you want to focus on are the ones that involve the most severe penalties for your association for *not* taking action during the coming year, while also being amenable to association influence at what appears to be an affordable cost (of course, the cost may not be clearly understood until you explore possible strategic change initiatives to address an issue). For most change challenges, your association will be able to take some action, and so the highest-penalty change challenges should virtually always top your list of candidates for action. Using two of the above examples, you know that your association can afford to do something to lessen your board's frustration, and the price of not acting will be awesome. But your association might decide that it cannot tackle the international-ization issue—despite the opportunities for new members and revenues—because of the likely cost of building the staff expertise to do so successfully.

If you decide to tackle a change challenge with high political content (such as a frustrated, underperforming board), avoid dealing with another politically charged issue at the same time (such as an archaic volunteer structure).

Fashioning Strategic Change Initiatives

Strategic change initiatives are essentially action projects to address selected change challenges. In developing its strategic change initiatives, your association will employ the familiar, tried-and-true project planning process. The usefulness of the strategic change portfolio lies in the selection of the right challenges to address, not in action planning per se.

Each strategic change initiative consists of (1) a specific target to be achieved, (2) an action plan spelling out steps and deadlines, and (3) a budget specifying the resources (time and money) to carry out the action plan. Let's say, for example, that your association has selected as one of its change challenges the issue of an underperforming board. Two strategic change initiatives have been developed to address this issue:

1. Upgrading the committee structure by moving to three standing governance committees—planning, operational oversight, and

external/legislative relations—to replace a structure of eight nongovernance committees.

2. Expanding and diversifying board member composition by adding five seats for directors who are drawn from outside the industry or profession represented by the association.

The action plans to implement these two targets will specify the steps that need to be taken, the accountabilities, and the deadlines. The plans will also spell out the time and dollars required. For example, implementing new board committees might entail the following:

- Developing a profile of the attributes and qualifications committee chairs should possess.
- Appointing committee chairs.
- Assigning board members to committees.
- Designating a management team member as support team leader for each new committee.
- Assigning other staff to serve on the support teams.
- Developing clear guidelines for committee operations.
- Orienting members on the role and functions of their committees.
- Staging the first committee meetings, at which priorities and work plans for the coming year will be developed.

Implementation of the new committees will most likely involve modest dollar amounts but will demand significant staff and board member time. The action plan must, therefore, be carefully paced to avoid overextending either board or staff members. Better to phase in new committees over a two-year period than rush the process and risk its falling apart mid-stream.

The Development Process

The nature, magnitude, and complexity of the change challenges your association chooses to tackle will determine how you fashion the strategic change initiatives to address them. The following guidelines have proved effective for many associations:

- Board members themselves should be intimately involved in fashioning strategic change initiatives related to the board's role, structure, and leadership. Perhaps the board can develop broad change initiatives in a retreat setting, after which staff or a consultant can fashion the detailed initiatives. Then the board or its executive committee should review the initiatives in detail and formally adopt them.

- Task forces consisting of staff and volunteers are a powerful device for fashioning strategic change initiatives. Some rules for task forces include:

  - Gear the composition of the task force to the particular change initiative being addressed; involve people who have the requisite knowledge and expertise and whose ownership will be essential for implementation. For example, a task force that is tackling the issue of low staff morale probably will consist solely of staff, perhaps with the addition of a human resource consultant. A task force that is working on the dramatic decline in annual conference attendance should include a number of nonboard members as well as staff.

  - Appoint task force chairs who bring the requisite credibility, interest, expertise, and leadership skills to the job.

  - Provide the technical support necessary to ensure task force effectiveness, including assistance in arranging meetings, developing materials, and following up on meetings.

  - Monitor the task force process to ensure that it is running smoothly. You might designate a member of the management team to serve as the coordinator of the task force planning process, use the management team as a monitoring and coordinating body, and review progress regularly with a board steering committee (often the executive committee).

  - Build in reviews of task force work at key points, involving both the management team and the board's steering committee.

- Strategic change initiatives should be reviewed and adopted by both the management team and the board before they are formally added to the strategic change portfolio. This often is accomplished at an operational planning work session involving the board and management team six months or so after the strategic work session that kicks off the annual planning cycle. This approach makes it possible to review strategic change initiatives in the context of all association operational priorities and plans for the coming year. The one exception would be initiatives related to the board itself, which need not be tied to the planning cycle.

Portfolio Management

Despite being well along the change road when your association's board has adopted well-crafted strategic change initiatives, the stretch of road between plans and action can be bumpy. The distractions of day-to-day operations, including unanticipated events and crises, always threaten to draw attention, time, and money away from your strategic change initiatives. In addition, resistance to change among board members, other volunteers, and staff—both conscious and subconscious—is an always-present hindrance.

How can you as CEO ensure that your association realizes a full return on the time and money invested in building its strategic change portfolio? You can help your association put in place a "strategic change program" to manage the change process and to protect it from the pressures of daily operations. You can also play a visible, active role in fostering commitment to the program and combating resistance.

Experience in both the for-profit and nonprofit sectors has taught us that large-scale change can easily be swept away by the powerful currents of day-to-day operations. To prevent this from happening, individuals and organizations must create a special structure dedicated to managing change. A kind of organization within the wider association, this strategic change program involves the participation of board members, other volunteers, and staff wearing their "change hats"—separate from their day-to-day responsibilities and roles. The program should consist of mechanisms for policy oversight, monitoring, coordinating, and replanning.

Many associations have involved their boards in strategic change programs by having their executive and other standing committees monitor the implementation of strategic change initiatives. The executive committee typically takes responsibility for overseeing implementation of any initiatives related to board structure and process (say, diversifying board composition and implementing new board committees). The board's planning committee might oversee initiatives related to new programs, services, and customers. The operational oversight committee would pay attention to initiatives related to internal systems enhancements (say, a new management information system) and the external relations committee to initiatives related to image, marketing, and volunteer involvement.

The CEO and management team should meet regularly to monitor progress, make planning adjustments, and resolve issues. When such meetings of the program steering committee occur, they are kept completely free of day-to-day operational matters. A key tool for carrying out their role fully is a comprehensive program implementation plan that lays out all of the initiatives side by side, so that required resources and interrelationships are easier to understand.

Whenever possible, the task forces that developed particular strategic change initiatives should be retained to manage their implementation. Task force chairs are often asked to serve on a technical coordinating committee, which reports to the program steering committee (members of the management team).

Since unanticipated events frequently occur, ensure your association's strategic change program has a built-in mechanism for revising strategic change initiatives. The implementation task forces, technical coordinating committee, and program coordinator should be primarily responsible for initiating and accomplishing such replanning, and the coordinator should secure the approval of the steering committee.

Several associations have enhanced the visibility and legitimacy of their strategic change programs through devices such as:

- Designating a particular conference room as the program "war room." An enlarged version of the implementation plan is hung on the wall, and the room hosts meetings of the steering and technical coordinating committees.

Tying It All Together

Many association CEOs have found it useful to designate a member of the management team to serve as the strategic change program coordinator. He or she is responsible for hands-on direction and coordination of implementation matters and for providing executive support to the board's committees and the management team in carrying out their oversight and monitoring roles.

Attributes of successful coordinators include:

- A strong commitment to the strategic change program.

- A passion for, and substantial skill in, project management, including a willingness to get involved in nitty-gritty implementation details.

- Strong technical planning skills; revising of strategic change initiatives is frequently necessary as the process moves forward.

- Easy access to the CEO and credibility among board and staff members; this is not a mere administrative support role.

- Substantial human relations and facilitation expertise.

One of the coordinator's most important jobs is to develop the comprehensive program implementation plan and to secure the steering committee's approval.

- Providing board members, staff, and volunteers with regular progress bulletins printed on special program letterhead.
- Creating a program logo that captures the spirit of positive change.
- Issuing to all participants a three-ring binder for all program documentation—plans, bulletins, minutes of meetings, and the like.

At this point you may be thinking, "This sounds like more time-consuming bureaucracy and real overkill. I already spend enough time doing bureaucratic things." The fact is, by putting a simple, dedicated structure in place to manage implementation of the initiatives in your association's strategic change portfolio, you will save considerable time. Instead of numerous ad hoc meetings to deal with problems and issues as they pop up, your association will have a mechanism for efficiently dealing with all of the details of implementation.

More important, your association will succeed in implementing valuable change in a timely fashion, thereby beating the odds and reaping the benefits in terms of a healthier, growing association.

Building Commitment, Countering Resistance

People look to your behavior as CEO more than any other factor in assessing the importance of planned change. If you continue to be fully engaged in program affairs—chairing regular meetings of the program steering committee, meeting frequently with the program coordinator, and being in command of the change process in public settings—then board members, volunteers, and staff are far likelier to consider the program a high priority and be committed to implementation of initiatives.

By contrast, if you largely disappear from the program scene soon after the initiatives have been adopted—participating infrequently in key committee meetings, being less accessible to the coordinator—then board, volunteer, and staff commitment will erode.

Here are several steps you can take to build commitment and counter resistance among board members, staff, and volunteers.

Be fully, visibly engaged in program affairs. The CEOs who are most effective at leading change, for instance, make a point of attending task force meetings frequently to keep their finger on the pulse of change. They stay for the whole meeting, rather than making a ceremonial appearance and then charging off to deal with more important matters.

Keep everyone's sights set high. Change—no matter how sorely needed and carefully planned and managed—can be brutal and dispiriting to people toiling in the ranks. Initial euphoria can easily give way to fatigue and depression unless you, as the CEO, continuously remind people in your association of the ultimate purposes and ends that give change its legitimacy and inspire commitment. If you help your board, volunteers, and staff keep their sights set high, you battle the perception of change for change's sake and make the inevitable pain of changing easier to bear.

Guard against volunteer and staff overextension and burnout. You are in a position to see everything going on in both the operational and change streams of the association, and you have the power to shape priorities and add or reduce burdens. Staff are particularly vulnerable to overextension because they have less power than board members or volunteers to protest and strong incentives to suffer quietly.

Merely adding the demands of change onto an already full agenda without making any adjustments is sure to kill enthusiasm and erode commitment. To take this path says this to participants in the change process: "I as your CEO don't take these initiatives seriously since I am not allowing you enough time to participate in implementing them. And I obviously don't care about your feelings since I am putting you in the position of having to juggle impossible priorities."

Such insensitive overloading often happens with CEOs who are type A personalities and believe that people respond to being pressured. If you want to see significant planned change implemented in your association, make the effort to reconcile operational and strategic change program demands so that the pace of change is reasonable. One way to do this is to involve your management team (convened as the program steering committee) in reviewing and reconciling the demands of day-to-day operations and the strategic change program.

Ensure full and open communication. Speak frequently in public settings about your association's values and vision and their connection to the changes being implemented. Explicitly link particular values and vision elements to certain strategic change initiatives.

For example, remind everyone that revamping volunteer involvement structures is not being done to satisfy some abstract organizational theory. Rather, it is to honor the value of strong, meaningful volunteer participation in association affairs and to realize the vision of an association with a committed, involved membership.

You will occasionally hear someone citing the "need to know" principle of communication, which holds that your board members, volunteers, and staff should receive only the information they need to know to carry out their specific duties.

While this may be a useful maxim for reducing the paper flow in your association, in the realm of change it makes no sense. In fact, the more people know about what is going on during times of change, the higher their spirits and the lower their anxiety will be. Feeling "in the dark" is one of the most common reasons that people resist change. So you as the CEO need to make sure that open, detailed, candid communication at all levels in your association is a characteristic of your strategic change program.

Board members, volunteers, and staff need to know what has been planned and how implementation is going—in detail—if they are to feel comfortable with the process. This is one of the easier requirements to satisfy, through such devices as frequent face-to-face briefings on program progress and informative newsletters that come out biweekly or monthly.

Provide opportunities for volunteers and staff to raise issues and share concerns. You cannot combat the fear of change through exhortation, which will merely drive the fear underground, where it will become more insidious. What you can do is provide staff and volunteers with frequent opportunities to raise questions and share their concerns about planned changes.

The most effective approach is to lead regular discussion forums, at which people feel safe enough to raise concerns without risk of punishment. Your behavior in such forums will be the critical determinant of their success. If you really listen and seriously respond to concerns, without verbally biting off people's heads or stridently defending decisions that have already been made, then people will feel freer to speak up.

When concerns are valid, make sure to adjust the strategic change program in response; otherwise, it will soon be obvious that the forums are purely cosmetic. If you don't believe that a concern is valid, explain your position clearly at the time, rather than appearing sympathetic and misleading people.

Empowering and Inspiring Your People

WITHOUT A DOUBT, the CEO is the point person in building an association's leadership and management capacity and in empowering an association's people. Unless the CEO is truly committed to, knowledgeable about, and highly skilled in these areas, significant association progress will be impossible.

In theory, an association's board sits in the ultimate driver's seat; in practice, the CEO has no peer in being able to influence association development. The board's capacity to govern and its capacity to lead and manage change are critical to surviving and thriving in a turbulent world. Both deserve considerable time and attention from the CEO. In addition, the CEO has a role in empowering and inspiring an association's people—its board, management team, staff, and volunteers—primarily through leadership in the design and facilitation of association processes and also through inspiration aimed at fostering trust and loyalty. These critical leadership skills are not mutually exclusive; the most successful association CEOs tend to be masters of all three. But they are quite different.

Process design and facilitation are technical skills that can be learned relatively easily. (See Chapter 4 for information on the psychological dimension of the art of facilitating.) By contrast, inspiring people, while it does involve developing technical rhetorical skills, has more to do with values-based behavior than words. It moves into the realm of character.

Although substantial evidence indicates that people's characters can develop, even after reaching the CEO's office, established character traits are notoriously difficult to change, primarily because they have to do with your psychological makeup (both your conscious and unconscious mind). Making the character terrain even more difficult to traverse is the debatable nature of values themselves. However, there is really no choice but to deal with values and psychological makeup, no matter how imprecise and debatable the concepts, since their impact on CEO leadership can be tremendous.

The Power of Empowerment

You hear the term "empowerment" a lot these days; indeed, it's almost become one of those buzzwords you have every right to feel skeptical about. The problem is that many people think of empowerment as both an ideological slogan and an essentially political process—the organizational version of "power to the people." Politics and slogans aside, empowering the people in your association—your board, management team, other staff, and volunteers—can help to make your association far more effective. But you must approach the job consciously and take it very seriously.

Empowerment, one of your preeminent responsibilities as a CEO, means that the people in your organization are able to:

- Fully apply the intelligence, skills, expertise, experience, talents, and other resources they possess in contributing to the achievement of the association's vision and mission.

- Participate in a meaningful fashion in determining association values, vision, mission, directions, and plans. The precise nature of that participation depends on their roles and responsibilities in the association.

- Grow more capable in terms of their knowledge, skills, and expertise as a result of their participation in association processes.

Participation and capacity building are not ends in themselves. Serious empowerment produces two major benefits for associations. First, higher quality decisions and plans result from meaningful participation of an association's people. Diversity and inclusiveness are obvious benefits in these complex, rapidly changing times, which place a premium on wider perspectives; heightened creativity; and systematic, regular innovation. As people grow more knowledgeable and capable through their participation, they contribute more powerfully to decision-making systems and processes.

Meaningful participation produces a spin-off that is a powerful force in human affairs: *ownership.* It has been proven time and again that the feeling of ownership comes from playing an important part in creating the association's products and making the decisions. Audiences for someone else's work are typically not owners of that work; that which is not owned, to a large degree, is not likely to be supported with passion. You should not count on exhorting board members and staff to own what they have played little part in creating, no matter how keen your rhetorical skills.

Paths to Empowerment

Truly empowered people not only participate in association processes, such as planning and budgeting, but also do so in a fashion that fully uses their resources. They actually influence directions, becoming more knowledgeable and capable as a result of their participation. By far the most powerful way to empower people is through your design and facilitation of association decision making, management systems, and processes.

Also important, but considerably less powerful, is the use of formal education and training. This contributes to empowerment only when it is tied to the current planning and management processes of the association.

Unfortunately, a historical tendency of leaders to over-rely on formal education and training that is not explicitly connected to actual association processes for setting directions and making decisions has probably generated far more frustration and cynicism than real empowerment. The classic example is an educational retreat aimed at enhancing people's creativity and sensitivity: The staff gather in a sylvan setting with a facilitator, accomplish demanding physical feats (scale a cliff), build trust (fall into each other's arms), and lower communication barriers (dare to tell what they really think about one another). In a truly ambitious retreat, participants actually unleash creativity (dare to choreograph and perform an interpretive dance before everyone).

Cavorting in the woods from Friday evening through Sunday afternoon can be deeply moving and educational and certainly enhances the potential for altering association life for the better. But all too often when Monday comes—and it always does—newly sensitized, better-educated staff find the same old organizational processes waiting for them. A few days back in the proverbial salt mine are typically all it takes to erase the warm glow that the weekend produced. The bad taste can linger far longer and can impede future efforts to involve staff.

Designing Participatory Processes

More than any other skill, empowering people requires that you learn to design participatory planning and management processes for your association. While you cannot expect to make all of the technical design decisions for a complex process, such as strategic management, you must ensure that a participatory design process takes place, and you must keep your hand in the process. Otherwise, you will put your association in danger of overinvesting in a technically fancy (and usually expensive) management innovation that may fall short of its promise and dash expectations. Think, for example, of the fate of total quality management experiments in the past few years. In many cases, the harm in terms of lowered morale, if not downright cynicism, has far outweighed the benefit of such ballyhooed panaceas.

In your capacity as chief process designer for your association, you will lead your board and staff members through the following key steps for any particular association system or process:

- Determine the impacts, outcomes, and products that the system or process should produce.

- Map out the key elements and steps in the process, including the nature of board, staff, and volunteer participation at each point in the process.

- Determine the resources required to implement the process and explicitly budget them, including technological support; board, staff, and volunteer time; needed knowledge and skills; and out-of-pocket expenses.

- Develop an implementation plan that will ensure that the design actually works in practice.

If you are truly committed to empowerment, you will want to involve your association's people in some appropriate fashion in designing the systems and processes that will empower them; this is what I call "empowerment." For example, the management teams of many associations in an annual retreat select which systems or processes they believe need to be redesigned and accomplish the fore-going design steps in broad-brush fashion. Afterward, staff task forces complete the detailed design, with close oversight from the CEO and management team.

When it is relevant, board members can also participate productively in the design process. For example, many board planning committees play a hands-on role in reviewing planning process design elements; they determine the most appropriate points for in-depth board involvement in the planning cycle before it is adopted.

Some association boards also allocate time at their annual strategic work session to identify aspects of the board's governance structure and process that appear to need serious redesign and appoint task forces to work out the details. Task forces may be employed to redesign the processes of filling board vacancies, monitoring board member performance, and developing board member leadership capacity.

The Design Process at Work

Let's take as an example of the design process at work one of the most powerful of all association processes in terms of potential impact: planning. The planning process encompasses both development of the strategic change portfolio (commonly called strategic management) and preparation of the annual operational plan and budget. The following description of the design process draws on the successful experience of several national associations:

1. Planning Process Outcomes. Without specific outcomes to aim for, planning process design can fall prey to preconceived notions and pet solutions. To avoid jumping to premature conclusions about process, develop a detailed list of outcomes the process is intended to produce. Some associations involve the whole management team in fashioning outcomes in a retreat setting or assign the job to a planning process design task force accountable to the management team.

Either way, the planning process can produce two kinds of outcomes: (1) substantive and content-related (for example, a mission statement, list of change challenges, or set of operational objectives)

Real-World Outcomes

Here are examples of planning outcomes that associations have identified to drive their planning process design, moving from the strategic to the operational sides of the spectrum:

- Clear, detailed values, vision, and mission statements to drive planning and to educate and inspire our members and the wider world.

- Selected strategic issues or change challenges on which to focus special attention.

- Change projects (strategic change initiatives) to make up our strategic change portfolio.

- Operational mission statements for each of our major operating divisions and programs. These statements clearly spell out overall purposes, functions, and beneficiaries.

- Detailed, measurable annual operational targets for each of our operating divisions and programs.

- Board involvement in the planning process that makes the best possible use of the board as a resource while building board ownership, interest, and enthusiasm.

- Staff involvement in planning that strengthens capability, builds knowledge and accountability, and promotes loyalty and enthusiasm.

- Association members who understand what our association is all about and who feel a strong sense of identification with and commitment to our association.

- Key stakeholders and a wider public who understand and feel supportive of our work as an association.

and (2) process spin-offs (such as *esprit de corps,* education, or a feeling of ownership).

2. Structural and Procedural Elements. With a set of desired outcomes at hand, you and the management team can design the planning process and structure. Involve the board's planning committee in signing off on the key elements; it should pay special attention to points of in-depth board involvement.

You might use an annual strategic work session or retreat to kick off the annual strategic management and operational planning/budget development processes, producing both substantial outcomes and process spin-offs. Many associations also stage an operational work session later in the fiscal year. At that time, heads of the association's operating divisions and major programs present to, and discuss with, either the whole board or its planning committee, specific operational targets for the coming year, important policy issues, and anticipated major expenditure increases. This occurs before preparation of the detailed line-item budget.

Such a session provides an opportunity for serious, substantive board input into operational planning that could not be achieved by thumbing through a finished budget document at the end of the planning cycle. It can also function as a powerful executive development tool for the staff involved, who hone their skills in making executive presentations and in dealing with board members.

Also important is the design of the planning documents themselves. For example, to build public understanding and support, you might publish your updated values, vision, and mission statements; change challenges; and newly adopted strategic change initiatives in a strategic plan. In addition to the detailed line-item budget that is essential for control purposes, you can publish an executive summary for key stakeholders and the wider public. It would communicate the association's operational priorities and performance targets, along with an analysis of revenue and expenditure trends.

3. Implementation Concerns. Whenever redesign of any facet of your association's planning process involves significant changes in structure (such as adding an annual retreat) or procedures, make sure that your management team (with approval from the board's planning committee) develops a detailed implementation schedule that pays special attention to major resource requirements.

For example, both board members and staff may require orientation and even training in the basic elements of the strategic management process before they can effectively participate in the retreat that initiates the process and in subsequent strategy formulation. Careful attention often has to be paid to

Not All Are Equal

In the real world, you can't expect all of your association's board members, staff, and volunteers to equally participate in every step of an association process, such as planning.

Here is a practical guideline that some associations have found useful in designing participation in their processes: Participation must be tailored to formal roles, authority, accountabilities, and capacities (such as perspective, experience, knowledge, expertise). The pre-eminent rule is that as many people at as many levels in the association as feasible should be involved, in as much depth as possible, in any step of the process—as long as their input is likely to be important in accomplishing that step and achieving its desired outcomes fully.

One caveat: Such participation must be technically and politically feasible and manageable and cannot carry a significant risk of jeopardizing the effective implementation of the process. For instance, involving one hundred people in an annual work session may make the event too unwieldy to manage.

extraordinary time demands, such as properly preparing for a two-day strategic work session that has never been held before. Ensuring that such a session is successful may require finding a qualified facilitator, developing a detailed design with work session objectives and agenda, and preparing background briefings.

Key Participants

Among your board's most important responsibilities are updating the association's values, vision, and mission and selecting the issues on which your strategic management process should focus. Your board is uniquely qualified to participate in-depth in this process, and this responsibility cannot be delegated. To involve the board in reviewing values, vision, and mission statements prepared by staff, for example, would trivialize board involvement. And experience shows that one of the best vehicles for carrying out this strategic responsibility is an annual work session involving key staff members. This is by its very nature a top-down process, and only so many people can be involved in a retreat without making it too unwieldy to manage. (I have seen retreats involving one hundred participants work, but with great difficulty.)

In designing the annual retreat involving the board, CEO, and management team, you will want to ask: Who else can I involve to enhance input and produce more process spin-offs without too great a risk of breakdown?

One association invites to its annual retreat the chairs of several policy and technical advisory bodies consisting of member volunteers, as well as representatives of key stakeholder bodies. Others have designed follow-through participatory devices, such as reviewing draft values, vision, and mission statements with focus groups of members in different parts of the country. They then consider that feedback when finalizing the statements for board adoption.

Another well-tested device for expanding and diversifying participation in planning is to require that division and program heads hold intensive planning sessions with their teams. In these sessions, all team members develop the annual operational performance targets and extraordinary expenditure requirements. Of course, it would be too unwieldy for all staff to participate in the ultimate work session, at which division and program heads present the targets to the board or its planning committee.

Almost nothing can kill the credibility of a process such as planning faster than designing participation that turns out to be essentially meaningless in practice. And nothing can erode morale faster. Despite this, I have witnessed countless instances when people have been put through the motions of participation for no serious purpose. Perhaps the most common example is the review of near-finished documents, which is often designed as more of a selling than a planning experience. In the first place, if a document has been largely finished, whether it is a vision statement or a set of operational priorities, there is probably little that can be done with it without causing disruption. So, reviewing such documentation is more likely to produce understanding and perhaps commitment (that's unlikely) than altered content, much less ownership. A reliable golden rule to follow is: Ask only for input that you seriously intend to use in important ways. If you ask for advice, you are well advised to take it, or be prepared to explain why not!

The CEO as Chief Facilitator

If they are to work well, association processes—especially when they result from a major redesign—often require skillful facilitation. This fine art requires sophisticated techniques for leading without commanding; for building and maintaining consensus, and hence enhancing the political viability of a process; and for capitalizing on the strengths that people bring to the process, thereby empowering them. The newer and more complex the process, the stronger the need for effective facilitation, which must deal with unfamiliar techniques as well as natural human resistance to change.

As CEO, you must learn to:

Facilitate at key points in the newly designed process, where your visible, positive involvement is essential to its credibility. For example, let's say you have signed off on a redesigned operational planning process; it involves division and program heads presenting their proposed performance targets to the management team for review, discussion, and revision before submitting them to the board's planning committee. If this is a dramatic departure from past practice, the management team may feel awkward or confused about such a review session. Perhaps team members will doubt that their input is truly desired or that any revisions will really result. This is a situation ripe for skillful facilitation that only the CEO can provide. So you have to prepare to play this role effectively, knowing that you can destroy the process before it is institutionalized, by such behavior as taking over the review yourself, putting people down, or cutting people off.

Ensure capable facilitation is provided in cases where you would not naturally, or could not be expected to, serve as the facilitator yourself. For instance, no CEO would want to facilitate his or her association's strategic work session for board and management staff, a highly complex and politically sensitive event. Instead, you want to ensure your board makes a sensible decision, such as retaining a respected professional rather than having a board member serve as the facilitator.

Effective Education and Training

You can do more harm than good by putting your staff or board through a high-level educational experience that raises their expectations about participation, only to dash heightened expectations in practice. Let's say that you send several board members to a national workshop on governance that focuses on the contemporary approach to proactive board leadership. You also send several senior staff members to the Center for Creative Leadership for a course aimed at expanding their capacity for creative thinking and problem solving. When your board and staff members return from these educational experiences, they'll be primed to participate in ways that use their newly acquired learning. You disappoint them at your peril!

A truly fail-safe approach is to make sure education and training is not done in isolation from real association needs and requirements. Many associations make the design of their boards' education and training programs an explicit responsibility of the executive committee. When planning the board's annual education and training program, that committee considers the needs associated with planned changes in the design of board structure and process. For example, putting a new standing committee structure into operation will almost certainly require that members of the new committees attend a formal orientation that is carefully planned and delivered.

Many associations actively involve their management teams in identifying and addressing major staff education and training needs tied to process redesigns. For example, if division and program heads will present performance targets to the management team and eventually to the board's planning committee, a training session on developing and giving presentations may make sense.

Keep in mind that on-the-job training is likely to have a deeper, longer-lasting influence than externally packaged approaches. Boards typically learn to make strategic decisions effectively by participating in a well-designed and facilitated strategic work session, not by attending a formal course on decision making. Management team members learn to design and deliver effective presentations to the board by actually going through the process of developing and presenting, rather than sitting through a training session. In fact, it is probably no exaggeration to say that your association's internal education and training efforts will be more effective to the extent that they are self-designed and self-delivered through on-the-job experience.

Being the Chief Inspirational Officer

People's loyalty and commitment to your association will grow through their participation in well-designed association processes that capitalize on their intelligence, experience, skills, and talents to produce significant outcomes.

However, you, in your capacity as the chief inspirational officer of your association, can also build trust and loyalty among your board and staff members and your volunteers. You can inspire people rhetorically—through carefully chosen and skillfully articulated words that direct their attention to, and explain the meaning of, broad association values, purposes, and ends. You can inspire people more powerfully by behaving in ways that affirm and reinforce certain universal core values and by making sure that organizational processes also reinforce the officially adopted core values of your association and in no significant ways contradict these values.

Words Do Count

Words can be a powerful association building tool. You are in a unique position as the CEO to raise people's sights beyond the day-to-day trials and tribulations of life in the trenches, by providing them with a context that gives deeper meaning to their labors and helps to replenish their stock of energy. People do care about values and vision, and understanding ultimate purposes and ends helps them to persevere in carrying out the means, getting them through difficult periods that might otherwise wear them out. In political history, this leadership role has been carried out splendidly at the national level by presidents such as Abraham Lincoln in the Civil War, Franklin Roosevelt in the Great Depression, and Ronald Reagan in the time of national drift after Viet Nam, Watergate, and the lackluster presidencies of Gerald Ford and Jimmy Carter. Of course, Messrs. Lincoln, Roosevelt, and Reagan were extraordinarily gifted orators. But you do not have to be uniquely gifted as a speaker to carry out your rhetorical leadership role successfully; doing so depends on your:

Choice of words. It is not enough to repeat the association's values, vision, and mission verbatim, merely reading to the assembled staff words created in a retreat and refined by the management team and board. Inspirational leaders take the time to translate noble concepts into terms their listeners can relate to personally. Franklin Roosevelt's stirring words from his first inaugural, "The only thing we have to fear is fear itself," took on more concrete, personal meaning through his fireside chats directed to people sitting in their living rooms around the country.

Suppose one of your association's core values is equal opportunity. If you can explain what this might mean in practical terms to a person who labors away in the accounting department, then you have a much better chance of inspiring loyalty.

Choice of venue. Perfunctory occasions have no place in inspirational communication. Words have greater impact when uttered in an intimate setting that makes it easier to personalize the purposes and ends being articulated. Equally inspiring are ceremonial occasions that dramatize and solemnize values, vision, and other higher ends, inspiring us by emphasizing their majesty and the ties that bind us all together, no matter what we do every day.

Experiment with both approaches. For example, discuss values and vision in informal division staff meetings, giving people ample opportunity to freely discuss your words and to make personal connections. Then hold an annual convocation-style meeting involving the board and all staff, to dramatize the common ends that unite both groups. Lincoln, Roosevelt, and Reagan were superbly skilled at the use of ceremony to lend majesty to national purpose.

Method of delivery. No matter what the setting, be careful how you articulate your words. If they are not heartfelt, you are unlikely to fool many people. And if lack of practice causes you to stumble during the presentation, you will communicate that your message is really not that important to you, and hence should not be taken seriously by anyone else.

People who use words effectively spend a lot of time practicing; the more practicing they do, the more "spontaneous" they sound. Most important, you must sound like you really do "care enough to send the very best."

Nothing Beats Behavior

As the CEO, what you do will, over time, mean more than what you say; if you don't walk the walk, people are typically savvy enough to know that it doesn't really matter whether you talk the talk. As the philosopher observed, perhaps exaggerating for effect: "Words are cheap."

Two kinds of CEO behavior have tremendous influence on people's trust, loyalty, and commitment. One is your personal, day-to-day adherence to core values in practice (or your violation of those values). The other is your guaranteeing that association processes promote, affirm, and in no major way contradict the values that have been articulated.

Thus far in this section, I have focused on officially developed and adopted association ideology in the form of values, vision, and mission statements. At a more personal level, your rigorous observance in practice of three universal core values—honesty, openness, and consideration for the feelings of others—will probably be more inspiring to those around you than any other behavior. Honesty means that you always tell the truth, and do not adjust that truth for different audiences. People learn that they can trust what you say, that your word is truly "good as gold." Openness means two things: that you do not deal in hidden agendas, deviously manipulating those around you; and you truly listen to and value the opinions of others. Consideration means that you respect the feelings of others, doing nothing that is intentionally cruel or will cause them needless pain and suffering.

This is clearly more than a little flag waving and bubbling apple pie, but paying close attention to your behavior where these core values are concerned can inspire trust and loyalty; significant, repeated violations can destroy trust and loyalty. However, you can be sorely tested and tempted to cut corners at times. Who has not shaped the truth somewhat to fit particular audiences? We call it "tailoring the message." The challenge is to draw the line at telling downright lies. The more rigorous your observance of these core values and the less you compromise them in practice, the more effective your leadership will be.

The organizational dimension of values harks back to your role as chief designer and facilitator of association processes. Your challenge is to ensure that officially adopted association values are promoted, and never violated in practice, by association processes. So if equal opportunity to advance professionally is a value, your system of job promotion actually embodies this principle in practice. If building people's capacity to lead and manage is an association value, then you ensure that people are involved in processes such as planning in ways that strengthen their leadership and management skills. If gender equity is a serious value, then the compensation system ensures that women and men are paid equally for the same work. If participatory management is a serious association value, then opportunities to participate are built into processes. If respect for the welfare of employees is a serious value, then the processes for determining operational priorities and setting the pace of work will guard against overloading and possibly burning out employees.

In addition to playing the chief process designer role, you must also take primary responsibility for ensuring that association processes are regularly audited to guard against violations of values and that when violations are identified, corrective action is taken. Repeated violations that contradict stated values are certain to erode both commitment and morale.

Leading with Your Total Intelligence

EXTRAORDINARY LEADERSHIP involves more than helping your board develop its capacity to govern, lead, and manage change, and it's more than empowering and inspiring the people in your association. There's a more personal aspect of leadership: your capacity to tap into—and put to work—the emotional and largely subconscious side of your intelligence that involves understanding and using your "heart." It also suggests how you might help your staff develop this critical capacity and put it to use in their work—for the ultimate benefit of your association.

Do matters of the heart have a valid place in any program to develop extraordinary CEOship and in leading and managing associations? Everything I have learned from study and real-life experience tells me the answer is an unequivocal yes. The most effective CEOs—those who deserve to be called extraordinary— draw heavily on the largely mysterious, irrational workings of the heart in leading their organizations. They have brought to the leadership task a keen awareness of the limitations of conventional intelligence, which protects them from the arrogance that can easily blind and hamstring bright, quick-thinking people in leading.

This is not the place to explore various psychological schools and theories on the matters of the heart, about which, by the way, there is considerable disagreement and often visceral debate. What I can do is point out the practical benefits of developing your heart intelligence and putting it to work for you in leading and provide you with some practical steps you can take in sharpening this critical—if hard to pin down—facet of your total intelligence. In doing so, I draw primarily on my work with hundreds of CEOs over the years, but also on my own struggles to expand my intelligence beyond the tried-and-true and oh-so-comfortable boundaries of conscious reasoning and discipline. My personal experience has certainly proved that old maxim, "No pain, no gain." And so, I cannot promise that this leg of your journey of growth will be a breeze; but I can guarantee you that it will be worth the effort, not only to you individually, but also to your association and everyone working with you.

Head and Heart Intelligence

Your movement up the ranks of association management probably has had a lot to do with your "head intelligence"—the mental endowment that people normally refer to in terms of IQ and "being smart." Your head intelligence relates to the processes of your conscious mind that enable you to fashion your philosophy and values and to reason logically; make well-thought-out decisions; solve problems; and produce priorities, directions, strategies, plans, and the like. Your head intelligence enables you to acquire knowledge and learn new skills and is also the source of such attributes as will, commitment, and discipline.

However much the workings of your conscious mind contribute to your success as a leader, they represent only part of your intelligence. You do not have to specialize in psychology or psychiatry to know that important mental processes go on in the part of your mind that is largely invisible to your head intelligence. This area is often called the unconscious, the subconscious mind, or the heart.

Understanding and being able to make use of your heart as an ally is a precious capacity I call heart intelligence. Heart intelligence, together with the workings of your head intelligence, make up the total intelligence on which your ultimate success as a leader and CEO depends.

Although developing the capacity to understand and use the wisdom of your heart in leading is more an art than a science, there are practical, tested ways of doing so. Just keep in mind that learning and applying techniques for building your heart intelligence may initially feel unnatural and uncomfortable, especially in the early stages of the process. If you have devoted your formal learning time to developing your head intelligence, you can relatively easily—and in straightforward fashion—learn to read faster, listen more attentively, solve problems with new logical techniques, and so forth.

You can't, however, think yourself into your heart. All the discipline in the world, combined with the keenest of reasoning, will not move you closer to understanding your heart. In fact, those attributes may drive you further away from understanding. This is one of the ironies of individual mental and psychological development: The most powerful tricks of the trade for beefing up your head intelligence won't get you anywhere with your heart intelligence.

So when we first venture into the mysterious realm of the heart on our journey of understanding, we find ourselves on unfamiliar terrain, with swirling fog and no comforting landmarks or guideposts. We often feel awkward and inept, and even endangered. In fact, for some people, the feelings of risk and danger are so strong that they cavalierly dismiss developing heart intelligence as "navel gazing" and "psychobabble." They could not be more wrong, but these people make up a large, vocal group. And, to make a complicated matter even tougher, not only are paths to understanding the workings of your heart less well mapped out than the ways of developing your head intelligence, you are likely to encounter another daunting barrier on the road to building your total intelligence: Your heart may actually resist being known by your head.

Many people experience this resistance as negative, irrational emotions of fear and anxiety when they attempt to gain access to their heart. These feelings can be intense, going well beyond the anxiety that people normally feel when learning something new. The feelings are, of course, real—but they are irrational in the head sense because there is no actual danger or risk to account for the intensity of the feeling. The feeling of danger can be so palpable that it stops your efforts to develop your heart intelligence cold. I will explore this powerful phenomenon in more detail later, but for now just know that, as you set off on the journey of building your total intelligence, you may find yourself tempted to flee for safety before you've traveled very far.

Getting To Know Yourself

Up to this point, you have done well professionally by relying heavily on your conscious knowledge and thinking skills. So why should you complicate your already hectic life by setting out on the journey of heart understanding—especially when you can expect some emotionally rocky times?

Here's the answer: To be a truly extraordinary CEO, you must have access to the treasures stored in your heart. You'll benefit by becoming:

- A more *creative leader.* Discovering attributes and qualities that define who you are in a fuller sense—and putting them to work—gives freer reign to the unconscious thinking process called intuition (the "ah-ha" phenomenon). The field of psychology has taught us that some aspects of your self can be stripped away from your consciousness early in your life; once rediscovered, they can enrich your leadership skills.

- A more *realistic leader.* You will learn to perceive the world around you with greater accuracy, through your firmer understanding and control of negative emotions that are based in your heart and that can distort your perceptions of reality. Your heart can be your head's indispensable ally in leading, but if you do not develop the capacity to understand your heart, your head can be tricked by these heart-based emotions.

Also, you will be able to develop a character trait of truly extraordinary leaders: *true humility.* This attribute will enrich your leadership by helping you attract and take full advantage of strong people with diverse skills and talents.

Our Many Faces

The heart is a treasure house of aspects of our self that are held in trust. These aspects help to define fundamentally who we are and who we could be. They are attributes and qualities, such as self-esteem, self-confidence, spontaneity, adventurousness, playfulness, humorousness, joyfulness, sexual expressiveness, artistic sensibility, intellectual curiosity, and trust, to name but a few. Whether the attributes that fundamentally define you are fully realized and expressed in your personal and professional lives depends on whether they remain in the consciousness (your head) and consequently can be developed. Otherwise, they remain latent and are but potentialities, and equally destructive, the emotions around them can lead to counterproductive behavior.

The term *persona* describes the faces people show to the world. Having a persona can serve a valid purpose in the workaday world, as a means of satisfying the expectations of board members, staff, and other people with whom we must maintain relationships. I learned the usefulness of persona some thirty years ago as a Peace Corps teacher in Addis Ababa, Ethiopia. Education was highly prized in Ethiopia, and students had a clear mental picture of a competent, serious teacher: dignified, distant (but not uncaring or cruel), demanding, and judgmental (but not capriciously so).

Many American teachers, raised in a culture that prizes informality and questioning, encountered problems as they tried to reach out to and befriend their new students. The teachers' personas often clashed dramatically with the expectations of their students, who could act out their disappointment quite violently. While lecturing one day, for example, I heard a commotion in the classroom next door. With suit jacket on, very much in command, I cautioned my students to keep quiet and looked out the door to see the neighboring teacher—a bright, earnest, loving, and truly likable American—bodily tossed out the door of his classroom!

Now, I am not really an uncaring or terribly formal person at heart, but, thankfully, I adapted my persona to the expectations of my students, at least in the early days. It made sense to do so, and I could not see any real violation of principle, just so long as I could figure out how to foster questioning and discussion without jeopardizing the control the students expected. Savvy CEOs learn not to be proverbial bulls in the china shop. They pay close attention to the culture of the association they have been appointed to lead and adapt their public face to it—at least closely enough to avoid offending their colleagues and possibly jeopardizing their support.

As long as they do not violate your values, the faces you show to the wider world are a valuable tool for leading. But this is true only when you have a complete understanding of who you are (total intelligence) and consciously know when certain sides of your self are not being expressed fully, if at all, through a particular persona that you have assumed.

Let's say that by nature—in other words, true to your real self— you are an iconoclast who takes pleasure in challenging established authority and the conventional wisdom and can apply an adroit and somewhat caustic sense of humor in toppling what you perceive as outmoded rules. You accept the CEO position at an association in chaos, one whose board, staff, and volunteers are exhausted, nervous, insecure, and hungry for order after a series of poorly conceived, slap-dash management innovations. If you are truly in command in the psychological sense, you will choose to subordinate your iconoclastic side for a time and assume the mien of a calm fatherly or motherly leader who promises stability. You know the time will come when letting your sense of humor show more fully will help you to be a more effective leader, but not now, when the need is for security and calmness.

Hidden Qualities

The problem comes when you are not even aware of qualities of your self that have been, for some reason, stripped away from your consciousness and that, consequently, cannot be put to good use in leading your association. They have become inaccessible to your head—hidden in your heart, which you can access only by developing and using your heart intelligence. In this situation, not only does your persona differ in significant ways from your real self, you are not even aware of the gap, and so there is nothing you can do about it. Qualities of your self that might make you a more effective leader cannot be put to use because they are unknown. And, there is ample evidence that your living with a persona that blocks out qualities (such as sensitivity) of your self that you do not even recognize can, over time, cause serious depression, which may hinder or even destroy your professional effectiveness.

It's been well documented that the stripping away of parts of your self happens in childhood, usually in the very early years, in response to some kind of emotional or physical pressure (which is often unintentional) from parents or other care givers. The process can be cultural as well—for instance, being pressured to meet the expectations of the community or society of which you are a part. To cope emotionally, a child's mind stores away the offending quality in the subconscious heart.

How well an attribute or quality that was once part of your conscious self is hidden in the heart and away from consciousness depends on two factors:

- The extent and depth of the pressure or abuse; and
- The original strength of the attribute or quality before it was stripped away.

Many male CEOs have had a tremendous problem letting the sensitive and caring sides of their natures—their "feminine" attributes, if you will—come through in their leadership. This limits their capacity to inspire loyalty. In every situation I have looked into, these CEOs learned in their childhoods to equate sensitivity with weakness and femininity. Many suffered terrible emotional abuse around such sensitivity and were told in actions and words that such feminine sensitivity was not only unacceptable but also could result in the removal of love and emotional abandonment.

I have also known CEOs—both women and men—whose sense of adventure and spontaneity was badly eroded in childhood at the hands of over-controlling parents and care givers. Taught in the emotional sense to live and work within narrow parameters—and not to challenge them at the risk of emotional abandonment—such unfortunate people bring less creativity to their work.

The emotional pressures and abuse that stripped away precious facets of who you are may not sound so bad now, from your vantage point as a forty-year-old executive, but go back far enough in your childhood and it felt like impending doom, even much like death to the then virtually defenseless child. Coping with this kind of emotional—not to speak of physical—abuse, a child's mind just gets rid of the offending quality by storing it away in the subconscious heart. That such things can and do happen all the time is truly sad, but there is good news: The qualities never really disappear. They can be rediscovered by your heart intelligence. And fortunately for those of you who resist the notion of parent bashing, you can reclaim and put to use once hidden attributes without having to hate your one-time abusers, although anger for a time may make sense, if only to help fuel your recognition and reclamation effort.

You can readily see how losing sight of important sides of your self—partially or completely—can constrict your persona and limit your effectiveness as a CEO. The humor, sensitivity, and artistic sensibility that are part of your true self cannot be enlisted fully to educate and inspire the people around you. Not being able to access the spontaneity and adventurousness that are part of your nature can prompt you to design planning processes that drive out creativity and to behave in ways that stifle initiative. Your inability to trust can lead you to over-control the people around you, keeping them from reaching their own potential and ultimately robbing your association of the full benefits from their contributions.

A Distorted View

This psychological drama is more intricate and convoluted than your merely losing sight of attributes that might make you a more effective leader. The emotions surrounding these heart-hidden attributes can actually distort reality, fooling your head into perceiving things that are not true.

This mental filter or distorting lens is one of the deadliest foes of effective CEO leadership. Here is how it works. Let's say that you as a child lost touch with your capacity to trust and to be spontaneous. These stripped-away attributes do not just sit in the heart waiting to be rediscovered and reclaimed. Emotions are generated around them, such as needing to control people and situations in order to feel secure. Or perhaps you feel danger when your control is threatened, either when you experiment with techniques that are not tried and true or when others raise challenging questions. Eventually the emotion (feeling threatened) grows separate from the need that generated it (for the safety that being in control brings) and from the sublimated attribute that is at the bottom of the whole thing (the freedom to be spontaneous and experimental).

The scenario I just described is the major reason why planning has been such an uncreative process. It is often why boards fail to develop into strong, creative governing bodies, even when the CEO intellectually grasps how to design and facilitate the planning process and board leadership development. Over and over again I encounter CEOs who talk the talk ("I really want a strong board." "We must produce innovation in our planning process.") but cannot manage to walk the walk. They actually sabotage their own efforts without being aware of what they are doing.

I once worked with a CEO who had fallen in love with participatory management and team building—so passionately that he talked incessantly about it and devoted thousands of dollars to education and training related to team development. Yet when he chaired executive team meetings, his need for dominance and control was obvious—to everyone but him—poor deluded fellow. He ranted and raved, cut people off mid-sentence, and constantly bemoaned the absence of people as smart and hard working as he. In short, he led by example in the Josef Stalin/Marquis de Sade mode. You can imagine how enthusiastically his department heads charged out to further the cause of participatory management and team building in the association. They did, however, pay verbal homage to the principles.

Projecting onto Others

Projection is another aspect of the distorting lens phenomenon at work. It happens in two basic ways: You turn someone in your life now into someone else from your past (the person reminds your inner child of that earlier acquaintance), or you feel strong, negative emotions about a person because you have projected onto him or her a trait of your real self that has been stripped away because it was unacceptable.

A common example is the man who has trouble dealing with strong, aggressive women. Many male CEOs have confessed to me they feel instantly defensive, combative, and often angry when confronted by a woman on the board or on their staff who appears to be challenging their authority. Usually, they have grown up with a highly demanding, critical, and perhaps emotionally abusive mother (who may be brought to mind when encountering an assertive woman).

A Personal Epiphany

None of us is immune to disliking someone who displays a trait that has been hidden away in our hearts because the trait is "unacceptable."

Not long ago, my wife, Barbara, and I attended a wedding reception, where the groom grabbed the microphone and quieted the guests. He proceeded—at length and very emotionally—to acknowledge some fifteen people who had shaped his life and contributed to his growth in important ways—mom, dad, teachers, coaches, friends. He was unabashedly emotional, choking up several times, and ended his soliloquy by hugging his mother and dancing with her to a sentimental ballad.

Was I moved? Hardly! I sat back with arms crossed, feeling quite superior to this guy who was the polar opposite of cool. He had bared his soul before the world, not having the good taste to keep his emotions under control in public. I cringed when, opening his arms wide, he declared, "Mom, I don't know what I would have done without your love."

A few days later, on a walk with Barbara, I laughed as I recalled and mocked his endless thank-you list. Suddenly I realized that I was skewering a man who had dared to show his heart in public—to be sentimental and to acknowledge that he couldn't go it alone. I was making fun of his lack of self-control, when for years I had been reading and writing about the need for men to break away from the facade of the cool, self-sufficient guy who keeps his emotions in check.

In fact, just a few days earlier, I had been telling Barbara about Dr. William Pollack's *Real Boys,* a book that gave me greater insights about my own struggle to break away from that deadening and limiting persona of the in-control male. Was it possible, I asked Barbara, that because deep in my heart I feared showing that side of myself that had so long ago been rejected, I projected onto the hapless groom the same rejection? Could my heart have tricked my head and distorted my perceptions?

Of course it did. And what was so amazing to me was how easily it had happened.

Others have talked of instantly becoming a ten-year-old boy again, on the inside, feeling a desperate need to protect themselves and go on the defensive.

Such distortions of reality prevent us from building positive, creative relationships with people simply because they remind us of someone who may be long dead, and certainly has lost any real power to harm. What makes this distorting phenomenon so insidious is that it often goes unrecognized. In such cases, the head is truly wrong-headed.

The Inner Child

The concept of the inner child may be a staple of the self-help literature, but it's still useful. Indeed, it is the best way to understand the distorting lens and projection phenomena.

Let's say that when you were just a child, you were shamed repeatedly about a trait that you soon learned not to display. It was stripped away from your conscious mind, no longer accessible to your head intelligence. In effect, as a child you learned to dislike or even hate an aspect of your self. The years passed, you grew up, and that stripped-away part of yourself is still largely unknown to you. Except you sometimes have a sense of sadness and incompleteness connected to the loss of that trait and you feel drawn to it; you also feel a keen sense of danger when you make any attempt to make the trait part of who you are today (because as a child you were threatened with scorn or worse for displaying it).

Think of those contradictory feelings—sadness, incompleteness, desire, fear—as belonging to that child of long ago, rather than treating them as dark and irrational emotions that you must fight, correct, or eradicate. Fear is the emotion we most love to hate because we rightly see it as a barrier to personal and professional achievement. But to consider fear as something "bad" to be overcome through discipline (as in "When the going gets tough, the tough get going") is ultimately a dead-end developmental street.

A surer path is self-understanding, self-love, and self-forgiveness. Acknowledge the child who is, for good reasons, feeling fear, and lead that child into the real world of today, where the danger no longer exists.

No Neat Packages

Perhaps the saddest and ugliest manifestation of the mental filter at work is stereotyping people into groups that we can abhor or hate in the abstract for their differentness: their race, their religion, their sexual orientation, their positions on hot-button issues. Hating appears easier to many people than thinking.

If a person is viewed through a stereotyping lens, which accentuates the negative and blocks out his or her real-life positive attributes, you squelch that person's opportunity to contribute to organizational success. Whatever the negative emotions underlying such stereotyping (which often comes with the turf of poor self-esteem), CEOs aspiring to extraordinary leadership should avoid it like the plague. At a national level, by the way, I am positive that stereotyping is a major reason for the growing volume of shrill rhetoric, bombastic placard waving, and the scarcity of civil dialogue on complex issues. Hating does appear easier to many people than thinking.

Especially be on the alert for stereotyping that is so second nature and undramatic in the moral sense that it goes unnoticed and unchecked. This is what is at work on clubbish, "birds of a feather" boards, which tend to replicate the good old boys and (maybe) gals when filling vacancies, without ever explicitly setting standards. Stereotyping is also at work when we surround ourselves with staff who fit a particular style, such as coolly competent, casually elegant, or easy to work with.

Being only with the people we feel most comfortable around comes at the expense of creative planning and decision making. It never fails that the person we feel we would have the hardest time relating to turns out to offer the most to our association; the packaging is an irritant, but the content is right. When packaging wins, substance suffers.

True Humility

One important character trait of highly successful leaders is true humility—the capacity to encourage, celebrate, take full advantage of, and foster the development of strength, assertiveness, and diversity in the people with whom you work. This is a critically important trait in these times, which demand of organizations, if they are to survive and thrive, that they master the art of leading, managing, and sustaining significant and creative change. The more people who are strong and of diverse skills, experience, and talents whom you can assemble and involve in making and implementing strategic decisions, the more likely your association is to generate creative and innovative strategies and hence to remain healthy and to grow.

People who are truly humble have healthy egos. That means the persona they present to the world (and which governs their interactions with others) incorporates three key attributes that draw on their well-developed heart intelligence:

1. Fundamental self-esteem and self-confidence, which rest on a foundation of self-love and keep you from being threatened by strong people and their challenges. No other person, no matter how bright, capable, or competitive, can shake your self-confidence and throw you on the defensive.

This does not imply that you must like every person you work with, enjoy their company, or feel comfortable with their style. It means only that at a "gut" personal level, negative feelings will not interfere with your making creative use of the resources they bring to the association. This does not mean that you must tolerate disloyal people, only that you stick with them as long as they are making a positive contribution and you can keep their disloyalty in strong enough check to prevent damage.

2. Realism based on the kind of self-knowledge that prevents negative emotions from distorting your perceptions of the people around you. Seeing through a clear, accurate lens, you do not fall into the trap of projecting a critical mother onto every strong woman you encounter or a punishing dad onto every challenging man. You are able to see people as they actually are, rather than as an emotion-laden symbol unrelated to their concrete reality.

3. Adherence to two core values: the belief that every person you encounter in life is a divine creation and hence deserving of your respect; and the belief that no person can be perfect, but all are capable of growth.

The former will help you find patience in interacting with others and will lead you to look for whatever unique contributions they might make to the association. The latter will save you from the self-righteousness that results in harsh judgmentalism.

Interestingly, true humility denotes strength, not weakness. It's the quiet strength built on a rock-solid character, not the loud, self-serving bombast and macho posturing that may result from self-hate and fundamental doubt about one's own value. Only if I doubt my own worth do I need to preoccupy myself with controlling the people around me, to prove that I am more worthy than they are, and to defend myself from their strengths.

The truly humble are anything but namby pambies; they tend to be high achievers who relish the race and run it to the fullest; they compete enthusiastically and take keen pleasure in victory. But victory to them lies in the achievement of their organization's ends, and they

Presidential Power

Perhaps the finest example of true humility in American political history is Abraham Lincoln, an intensely ambitious, self-made man in the Horatio Alger tradition. Lincoln developed a successful, lucrative career as a trial attorney in Illinois. He relished the rough and tumble of politics, and he became a superb stump orator who was a match for the finest debaters of his time.

Despite winning less than a majority of the vote in 1860, Lincoln gained extraordinary power during the course of one of the largest and most tragic wars in the history of the world to that time. But what strikes students of Lincoln's presidency—in addition to his firm adherence to the principle of national unity and his ability to articulate fundamental values in unforgettable prose—is his healthy ego. It enabled him to tolerate with amazing patience not only rambunctiousness in those close to him but also arrogance, rudeness, and even disloyalty.

This is not to say that Lincoln was a great judge of people. In fact, his track record in choosing generals was less than inspiring. It is not to say that he was especially skilled in human resource management, although he did have a way of charming people with his folksy humor. And Lincoln certainly wasn't a morally perfect person. On the contrary, he had his share of flaws, as he would readily admit.

It is to say that he never gave up on people unless they could not contribute positively or if their disloyalty had become too dangerous to tolerate. Lincoln was truly humble, but strong, and that is one of the most important reasons for the growing reverence we feel for him and the most important reason for looking to his presidency for powerful lessons in leadership.

fundamentally reject the notion that their achievements must be at the expense of those around them. The truly humble are "win-win" people who view others as potential contributors to be facilitated—even manipulated, if necessary—to ensure that the association realizes the fullest benefit from their contributions.

Developing Your Heart Intelligence

Character is not a set of immutable traits. People are always capable of dramatic change and growth in this area. Of course, long-enduring character traits can appear to be inborn just because they are so powerful and have been around so long we can't remember a time when they were not a part of who we are. To become an extraordinary CEO, you must challenge what appears inevitable and immutable in your character when it detracts from your leadership.

It is all too easy to say, "Who I am is who I am. So I easily go on the defensive when I am challenged; I can't remember ever not feeling defensive when people challenge me. Being the in-house prickly pear is one of my flaws that I just must learn to live with and work around."

This is an easy position to take because it rides on the back of a powerful beast—inertia—and conveniently saves you from the terrors and pain that inevitably accompany attempts to change in significant ways.

I am talking about changes in character that have to do with attributes and qualities of your self that can be understood through developing your heart intelligence and that generate emotions that can be dealt with effectively only if you use your heart intelligence to understand their cause and to gain some control over their impact.

What can you do to develop your heart intelligence and play a more conscious and powerful role in shaping your character? Here are three steps you can take.

1. Seek knowledge. Make an explicit part of your executive development strategy increasing your knowledge of the psychological processes at work in the sphere of your character development. This means treating your character as a precious resource in leading and its development as a serious professional issue. It also means that you believe in the necessity of continuing character development.

2. Seek quiet. The cacophony of day-to-day working and living can drown out the voices of your heart, which often speaks in whispers. At the very least, carve out a half-hour or hour every day, perhaps early in the morning before your spouse and children are up, to just sit quietly. Leave your mind as open as possible, and do nothing productive—don't think about the day ahead or reflect on issues and problems. If you plot out every hour of the day to do something, you may not hear your heart until you are in the grip of depression or anger.

If you have reason to believe that your heart and head are far from working together as allies—say, when you experience significant interpersonal problems at work or home—consider taking a more formal approach to listening. One of the most powerful is meditation, which can yield significant benefits in terms of heart intelligence while taking no more than an hour a day. Spending a day or even a week or more every year in a retreat setting, perhaps with a professional leader, is another way to enhance your heart intelligence. Given the power of the head and the demands of day-to-day life, something as dramatic as a retreat may be required to open up communication with your heart. Since you can know your heart through feelings and emotions, you want to pay close attention to your emotional life, monitoring and questioning your feelings, especially when they are intense, rather than shunting them aside or trying to overpower them.

3. *Seek understanding.* Be aware of, and thoughtful about, your emotions. Question their origins and attempt to understand them more fully, rather than trying to keep them in check (a common tactic when emotions such as fear are viewed as negative and a sign of unacceptable weakness). This is obviously an imprecise science, but merely being self-analytical about your feelings and emotions and repeatedly asking "What does this mean?" can build your heart intelligence.

Such self-centeredness—searching for your self in your heart as well as your head—often bothers people who have been taught that being inwardly focused is self-indulgent and selfish. But being self-centered in the sense of paying attention to your heart's signals and attempting to understand them is the opposite of self-indulgence. Indeed, it can be so uncomfortable and threatening a process that, in author Scott Peck's words, it tends to be a "road less traveled."

Let's say you are participating in a breakout group in a retreat, and you suddenly feel tremendously uptight and can hardly speak because your chest is so tight. Ask what is going on, and try to learn about your self from the experience. Or perhaps the thought of mounting the podium before an audience of two hundred people strikes terror in your heart. What does this tell you about your self? Where does this self-consciousness come from? Is it fear of failure, an intense need to appear perfect before others? Since, realistically speaking, your audience is unlikely to be harshly judgmental, what is the source of such intense emotion?

Away from the Hustle and Bustle

A few years ago, feeling somewhat empty and burned out, I scheduled three days at a Jesuit retreat center. Never having spent so much time alone with no clear aims (I even play seriously), I felt lots of anxiety about the impending event as it drew nearer. In fact, my anxiety grew so keen that I was on the verge of canceling (too much work, too busy, obligations to clients, and so forth). Fortunately, my wife goaded me to follow through.

It was a tremendously rewarding experience. The minute I began to walk around the grounds soon after arriving, my anxiety came clear: "You, my boy," I said to myself, "do not feel that you are worthy of any profound experience; you expect to feel nothing but rejection." Starting with what felt like a revelation about my character, the days unfolded peacefully and joyfully. I learned about my self more deeply than ever before. I merely regret that I find it so difficult to come up with the time for regular retreats.

I and many colleagues of mine who earn part or all of their living from professional speaking will testify that such fears are common and that attempting to understand rather than quash them is a reliable way to lessen their grip.

Gaining heart intelligence also means monitoring and questioning less intense, more diffuse emotions that can tell you about parts of your self that are hidden from your consciousness. For example, do you feel a sense of sadness or longing when you read certain passages, view certain art, or hear certain music? If so, ask yourself whether there is part of your self being preserved in your heart that promises the wholeness and happiness you long for if you can reclaim it, making it part of your conscious self and integrating it into your working and living. Now, it is possible that the message you are receiving is that you need to chuck your job and move to an island paradise, where you will live at last as you were meant to, painting masterpieces. But what about the possibility that you can less dramatically integrate once-hidden attributes of your self into your CEO leadership role, thereby leading more creatively and effectively because you are more spontaneous and theatrical or less inhibited and controlling? I will tell you this: People can sense when leaders are not being their true selves, and they tend to back away from such falsity.

The Language of Dreams

There can be no question that your heart can speak to you through dreams, and I strongly counsel you to take the time to think about and analyze any dreams that recur regularly, that are especially vivid, or that carry with them strong residual emotion. I do not want to carry this too far. There are surely dreams that speak randomly, with no particular symbolism worth trying to untangle, and I certainly do not recommend that you look for portents of the future or guidance in solving particular problems in your dreams. All I am saying is that you should be open to the possibility of occasionally gaining heart intelligence through dreams.

CEOs I have known and worked with have shared important dreams with me over the years that have impacted their lives and their leadership. Twenty years ago, I could not have imagined myself discussing dreams over lunch with a rough and tough CEO, but times have definitely changed, thank heaven.

A CEO I worked with not long ago shared two dreams that significantly affected his professional life. He was in the throes of beginning an ambitious new book that demanded a dramatic break from his past writing efforts, which had been largely dispassionate and tightly controlled. The night before he had scheduled himself to begin seriously writing again after several weeks' hiatus, his heart spoke to him in two vivid dreams that dealt directly with his dilemma and reinforced his commitment to bring greater passion to his work.

In the first dream, he was a music teacher who, with baton in hand, was setting up music stands and chairs in two small rehearsal rooms. The students were, strange to say, only infants dressed in nightgowns with blankets around their shoulders; no instruments were in evidence. He remembered feeling a sense of danger and foreboding, which didn't make sense in the setting (he loved music and had been student conductor of the concert band in high school).

In the dream, the CEO walked from one room to the other, where he picked up one of the infant-students and held her in his arms. Hearing a rustle, he looked around and saw that another child had entered the room. Picking up this newcomer, he noticed a wicked-looking carving knife in his hand, which he pushed away. Sensing a threat, he turned to the other child and saw a dagger plunging into his face. Waking up with a scream, he was so frightened that he couldn't go back to sleep for another hour.

Sound asleep again, he dreamed that he went to his car dealer to lease another car. He next remembers coming out of the car dealership with a plastic kiddie car about the size of a sled. He then found himself atop a tall tower, hundreds of feet in the air, sitting in the kiddie car with a young woman. He wanted to drive the car off the tower but felt tremendous fear. Suddenly—with a scream of joy—he and his young passenger hurled themselves into the abyss, and he awoke.

Thinking about these two dramatic dreams early the next morning, the CEO was certain that his heart was telling him in no uncertain terms to get going with the creative writing project, despite his fears. He interpreted the first dream—in which he was a music teacher threatened by death—as a message that his old directive and controlling self (hence, the baton) must die to allow his newborn creativity (the infant students) to emerge and flourish. The second dream seemed a less nightmarish affirmation: Throw caution to the winds and dive into the abyss with exuberance—with the complicity of the feminine side that had been shamed into hiding so long ago.

I could share countless other dreams that I have had and that have been told to me. The point is to pay attention to this means by which your heart can speak to you, divining what meaning you can, and your heart intelligence will grow keener.

Psychotherapy

Experience—mine and many others'—has taught me that working with a trained psychotherapist can be a valuable way to uncover and understand your heart's secrets and to reclaim valuable aspects of your self. For some reason, many people have come to think of psychotherapy as self-indulgent or weak, or—even worse—as treatment for the seriously mentally ill. I have learned over the years that psychotherapeutic sessions with a trained professional whom you trust is a sign of good sense, courage, and commitment to learning and growth.

When the body needs help, we have no compunction about seeing an internist. We make sure that our dental problems are dealt with by a dentist. We don't say, "Oh my gosh, people will think I'm really weak if I don't do that knee surgery myself or drill out my own cavities." Why would we not want to seek the assistance of a trained psychotherapist in dealing with the mysterious workings of the conscious and subconscious mind, at least on occasion?

Of course, you might not be attracted to weekly therapy sessions when you are not grappling with any dramatic psychological problems. But meeting occasionally with an expert to discuss intense emotions in your life can be useful for self-understanding. Keep in mind that you do not need to rely on one-on-one therapy exclusively. Many people have found group work valuable—for example, men's groups dealing with questions about masculinity.

A few years ago, I was diagnosed as having colon cancer. Looking back, with the cancer now gone, I see how imperative psychological preparation for surgery was in light of my type A personality and addiction to a grueling physical pace. Why didn't I anticipate the depression that descended after surgery and take steps to deal with it by working with a professional? No one in the medical community suggested it, and I had always been accustomed to toughing things out myself. Not bright, to be sure, but probably common.

Don't let yourself fall into the same trap. Treat matters of the mind as being just as important as matters of the body. Be open to the possibility of expert advice or even intervention when you feel too disconnected from your heart or overwhelmed by emotion.

Helping Others Find Their Hearts

Your responsibility as a leader includes helping the people around you understand the head–heart connection and strengthen their heart intelligence. Doing so will help them live richer, fuller lives and will enhance their contributions to the association you lead.

You are probably not a trained therapist, but you can take some practical steps to help people become smarter in the heart sense:

Spend time seriously talking about the subject in staff meetings and other forums. As the CEO, your words tend to pack a wallop. If you joke about such matters as being "flaky" or "squishy," you will be heard and do serious harm to the cause of heart intelligence.

Share your experiences in learning to hear and understand heart signals. People around you are likely to be deeply moved by your sharing fears and difficulties, rather than hearing you suggest it was smooth sailing all the way.

I will never forget the powerful impact a CEO made when she explained to her management team why she had launched an ill-conceived innovation. She revealed that she had a tremendous need to feel in control based on her childhood. Far from taking advantage of her candor and abusing her trust, her team gained greater respect for her leadership.

Behave day after day in ways that demonstrate your commitment to heart intelligence. Always encourage the expression of heartfelt thoughts, and never demean people for showing sides of themselves that do not fit a traditional model.

This is easier said than done. At a meeting a few years ago, before taking up the business at hand, several of us were casually chatting about movies. One participant began speaking excitedly about one of his favorite films and gesturing flamboyantly. Without thinking, I commented, "What are you smoking?" He immediately quieted down and stayed silent for the rest of the meeting. I put him down; I shamed him. Although I eventually screwed up the courage to apol-ogize before the group, the damage had been done.

A small thing, perhaps, but as a steady diet such behavior can be terribly destructive.

Keeping Informed

Y OU FACE TWO CHALLENGES in attempting to stay up to date in "CEOship." First, no such field exists. Rather, you'll find various more or less useful sources of information on this or that facet of CEO leadership. Second, you have precious little time to read, much less explore various sources, so your self-education efforts must be highly focused and selective.

This chapter suggests certain streams in the literature that you might profitably tap into to become—and remain—an extraordinary CEO. It's not intended as a comprehensive bibliography of books and articles pertinent to the subject of CEO leadership generally, or to association CEO leadership particularly. It assumes that you are already knowledgeable about the nuts and bolts of association management, such as financial planning, membership recruitment and retention, budgeting, and human resource management. If you do need to beef up your skills in a particular area, abundant sources of information are readily available in the ASAE catalog of publications.

Below, divided into four subject areas, are examples that I have found helpful in shaping my own understanding. Rather than attempting to provide an exhaustive list of publications in each of these areas, I instead offer illustrative examples with which I am very familiar and have found uniquely powerful in shaping my own

A Word About Periodicals

CEOs looking for useful information in periodical literature often find journals and magazines to be either highly academic and theoretical, with little obvious practical utility, or highly nuts and bolts, with slight theoretical value. You almost have to choose between the rarified heights or the trenches, with nothing in between.

One journal bridges the two camps consistently and successfully: *Harvard Business Review.* I have found it a fruitful source of powerful insights on leadership at the highest level, with balanced attention to theory and practical applications.

ASAE's *Association Management* magazine also marries theory and practice successfully, although it pays less attention to CEO leadership than *Harvard Business Review* and tends to confirm rather than advance developments in CEOship.

understanding. I assume that you can go out and find your own books and articles, using this essay as a helpful guide.

Governing Boards

The surprisingly small number of books on this important topic indicate the relatively minor place occupied by governance in the field of leadership and management, until fairly recently. One does not have to go back very far in the past to find books filled with little golden rules focusing on keeping boards quiescent and out of administrators' business (what I call the "be a good little board/slap on the wrist school" of governance). Only fairly recently have authors moved beyond narrow rules pertaining to dividing the turf between the board and CEO, into more interesting and useful explorations of how to develop boards that truly do provide strong leadership and how to build positive, productive board–CEO partnerships.

John Carver's *Boards That Make a Difference* (Jossey-Bass, second edition, 1997) was a path-breaker and still serves as a useful resource to any CEO who seriously wants to understand the role of the board in leadership. However, Carver's heavy emphasis on fashioning and maintaining a formal policy structure, while it rightly focuses board attention on ends rather than means, neglects the creative role of the board in leading innovation and change. Douglas Eadie's *Boards That Work* (ASAE 1995) draws on Carver's work in exploring in greater detail how the board can participate actively with the CEO and executive team in leading innovation. It also draws heavily on real-life association experience.

Consider becoming a member of the National Center for Non-profit Boards, which has published a list of practical, brief, and easy-to-read booklets on every conceivable aspect of board development and operation. The center also publishes a member newsletter that highlights practical issues related to nonprofit governance.

Innovation and Change Leadership

Strategic Planning and Management

As a field, planning has tended to focus more on achieving neatness and control than on producing serious innovation. Even so-called strategic planning has generally confirmed what already is and then projected it into the future. No wonder that strategic plans sit on shelves collecting dust, rather than serving as serious blueprints for innovation and change.

There is one comprehensive survey that deserves the attention of any nonprofit CEO who aspires to use formal strategic planning as a tool: John Bryson's *Strategic Planning for Public and Nonprofit Organizations* (Jossey-Bass 1995). My only problem with Professor Bryson's comprehensive, well-written survey is that it offers far more information than you really need on the subject and tends to bog you down in the details of the planning process. Innovation and change do not stand out as the preeminent reasons for doing the planning.

Over the past decade, a variation on the broad strategic planning theme known as strategic management has largely replaced strategic planning. It pays more attention to change as an objective and to the implementation of change. The process is described straightforwardly—with an association focus—in Douglas Eadie's *Meeting the Change Challenge* (ASAE 1996).

Change Management

As you look at resources in the field known as change management you will notice the tendency of books to focus on a particular element of the change process, without attempting to link them to an integrated process or system. By far, the most attention has been paid to implementing change, especially to overcoming resistance and getting people to go along with planned change. Many books of this genre focus on manipulative techniques and are little concerned with the content of change and its qualitative aspects.

One of the few books that offers a comprehensive approach to leading innovation and change in nonprofit organizations is Douglas Eadie's *Changing By Design* (Jossey-Bass 1997). It describes how to build and integrate three capacities that are essential for successfully leading change: board and CEO leadership, innovation, and implementation.

The Learning Organization

Although not addressing change leadership and management per se, books that deal with how to develop and lead what is known as the "learning organization" can help you understand what is involved in building innovative capacity. Easily the best known and most influential book of this kind is Peter Senge's *Fifth Discipline* (Currency-Doubleday 1994). Senge's descriptions of the core disciplines involved in building the learning organization, such as personal mastery and mental models, are must reads for any CEO dedicated to becoming an extraordinary leader.

More explicitly focused on innovation and change leadership is the work of Rosabeth Moss Kanter. Her *When Giants Learn To Dance* (Touchstone Books 1990) draws on industrial research and development experience to make a powerful case for managing innovation in a "newstream" process that is kept separate from mainstream operations.

A brilliant student of the cognitive process and the philosophical framework for strategic decision making, Nathan Grundstein, has written a powerful work on strategic thinking, *The Knowledge of Strategy* (Case Western Reserve University 1992).

Traits of Highly Successful CEOs

History

The fields of history, psychology, spirituality—and, to a lesser extent, management—are fruitful sources for understanding why certain types of leaders are successful. History, in the form of biography and autobiography, can be a rich source of practical wisdom about leadership. Relatively recent books that are well worth your close attention include:

- Katharine Graham's *Personal History* (Alfred A. Knopf 1997) and Colin Powell's *My American Journey* (Random House 1995).

- Ron Chernow's *Titan* (Random House 1998), which is a brilliantly researched and written account of John D. Rockefeller, a genuine business genius and philanthropist without peer.

- David Herbert Donald's *Lincoln* (Simon and Schuster 1995), which offers new insights into the character of Abraham Lincoln, vividly demonstrating the importance of values in leadership, and David McCullough's *Truman* (Simon and Schuster 1992), which through Truman's life, illustrates "true humility."

- Taylor Branch's amazingly detailed account of Dr. Martin Luther King, Jr.'s life in the early 1960s, *Pillar of Fire* (Simon and Schuster 1998), vividly depicts the power of vision to inspire change, when articulated with rhetorical skill and passion by a charismatic leader.

- Doris Kearns Goodwin's *No Ordinary Time* (Simon and Schuster 1994) demonstrates the power of vision in the hands of one of America's most charismatic politicians, Franklin Roosevelt. It also describes the unique partnership that Franklin and Eleanor fashioned to reinforce one another's leadership in their respective spheres.

- Deborah Shapley's enthralling *Promise and Power,* a life of Robert McNamara, former president of Ford Motor Company, secretary of defense, and president of the World Bank, tells a sad story of the limitations of so-called rational decision making and the all-too-fallible management information systems designed to support it.

Leadership

There is not really a field called leadership, but hundreds of books describe the characteristics of effective leaders. I strongly recommend the very readable and practical books of Warren Bennis: *Why Leaders Can't Lead* (Jossey-Bass 1989) and (with Bert Nanus) *Leaders: The Strategies for Taking Charge* (HarperCollins 1985). Bennis bases his work on extensive research on real-life leaders in a wide variety of fields. He hones in on such critical traits as being visionary, being able to communicate vision, inspiring through behavior that reinforces values, and possessing the capacity to facilitate participation and build ownership among staff.

A small, plain-spoken book filled with practical leadership wisdom by a highly successful CEO is Max De Pree's *Leadership Is an Art* (Dell

1989). Perhaps the best work on the subject of the role of values in leadership is James O'Toole's *Leading Change: Overcoming the Ideology of Comfort and the Tyranny of Custom* (Jossey-Bass 1995).

Among the most fascinating and thought-provoking works on leadership are those that fall in the intersection of biography and psychology. Howard Gardner, the director of Project Zero at Harvard's Graduate School of Education, has studied and written on leadership, not only of organizations but of domains of knowledge, from the perspective of a psychologist with a particular interest in the creative process. My work has been heavily influenced by three of his books: *Extraordinary Minds* (BasicBooks 1997), *Leading Minds* (BasicBooks 1995), and *Creating Minds* (BasicBooks 1993).

Understanding Your Self

If you hover around the psychology, spirituality, and self-help book shelves of major book stores, you will find works that will help you understand who you are more deeply than your conscious persona and will illuminate the powerful heart–head partnership.

In this regard, you may want to look at a masterful summary of Carl Jung's key concepts, June Singer's *Boundaries of the Soul* (Anchor Books 1994). Dimensions of the self are clearly and attractively described in James Masterson's *The Search for the Real Self* (Free Press 1988). Studies that look at the gender dimension of self-development can be very useful; for instance, William Pollack's *Real Boys* (Random House 1998) proves interesting and thought provoking.

My thinking on the subject of the heart–head connection and spiritual growth generally has been enriched by Scott Peck's *The Road Less Traveled* (Simon and Schuster, second edition, 1998), Thomas Moore's *Care of the Soul* (HarperCollins 1992), and Wilkie Au's *By Way of the Heart* (Paulist Press 1989).

Serious fiction, particularly novels, can also stimulate and facilitate self-understanding as you search for inspiration and illumination. To be honest, if heretical, I am more inspired and better informed on the workings of the head and heart by a serious work of fiction than many of the derivative "publish or perish" books that the field of management generates.

Three very different novelists, among the many I admire, have taught me about my place in my universe and the multiplicity of my self: Charles Dickens (who speaks about the pain of emotional abandonment through the metaphor of literal orphans, especially in *David Copperfield* and *Oliver Twist*); John Updike (especially the four Rabbit novels), who with a keen eye that misses no detail and gentle humor that illuminates our foibles without humiliating us, teaches us about the essential aloneness of human beings and our universal longing for meaning; and Aleksandr Solzhenitsyn, whose *The First Circle* is a fine account of the indomitableness of the human spirit in the face of evil tyranny.

Find your own inspiration, not only in works of fiction and poetry, but also in the dramatic and musical arts.

About ASAE Publications

THE AMERICAN SOCIETY OF ASSOCIATION EXECUTIVES in Washington, D.C., is an individual membership organization made up of more than 24,900 association executives and suppliers. Its members manage leading trade associations, individual membership societies, and voluntary organizations across the United States and in 44 countries around the globe. It also represents suppliers of products and services to the association community.

This book is one of the hundreds of titles available through the ASAE Bookstore. ASAE publications keep you a step ahead by providing you and your staff with valuable information resources for executive management, finance, human resources, membership, career management, fundraising, and technology.

A complete catalog of titles is available on the ASAE Web site at **http://www.asaenet.org** or call the Member Service Center at 202/371-0940 for the latest printed catalog.

About Doug Eadie

DOUG EADIE, founder and president of Doug Eadie Presents! and Strategic Development Consulting, Inc., is a national leader in helping executives to strengthen their leadership skills, organizations to innovate and lead change, and boards to develop into effective governing bodies. Doug has worked with thousands of board members and executives and over 400 organizations during the past quarter-century. He served as a founding member of ASAE's Executive Management Section Council from 1996 to 1998.

Doug is the author of ten books in addition to *The Extraordinary CEO*, including *Changing By Design* (Jossey-Bass 1997) and two other books for ASAE: *Boards That Work* (1994) and *Meeting the Change Challenge* (1996). He is a Phi Beta Kappa graduate of the University of Illinois and was awarded the Master of Management Science degree by the Weatherhead School of Case Western Reserve University.